Learning and Teaching with Interactive Whiteboards

Primary and Early Years

Learning and Teaching with Interactive Whiteboards

Primary and Early Years

David Barber
Linda Cooper
Graham Meeson

LearningMatters

First published 2007 by Learning Matters Ltd

British Library Cataloguing in Publication Data
A CIP record for this book is available from the British Library.

The right of David Barber, Linda Cooper and Graham Meeson to be identified as the authors of this work have been asserted by them in accordance with the Copyright, Design and Patents Act 1988.

Thanks are due to the manufacturers of Promethean ACTIVboard™ and the SMART Board™ products for the permission to reproduce screenshots of their software that they have extended to us.

We would like to thank the following colleagues and students on the BA Primary Education (QTS) course at Bishop Grossesteste University College for their enthusiasm and contribution to this publication. These include our colleague Ashley Compton, for the diagram on page 71 and information on the use of Excel, and also students Karen Broadbent, Louise Crowther, Kylee Morrell and Glen Durkin.

ISBN 978 1 84445 081 7

Cover design by Topics – The Creative Partnership
Project Management by Deer Park Productions, Tavistock, Devon
Typeset by Pantek Arts Ltd, Maidstone, Kent
Printed and bound in Great Britain by Cromwell Press Ltd, Trowbridge, Wiltshire

Learning Matters Ltd
33 Southernhay East
Exeter EX1 1NX
Tel: 01392 215560
info@learningmatters.co.uk
www.learningmatters.co.uk

Contents

The authors   vii

Introduction   ix

1 Technical introduction   1

2 Getting started   10

3 Software   19

4 The interactive whiteboard in school and in the classroom   31

5 Theoretical underpinnings and pedagogical themes   41

6 Finding, evaluating and using resources   51

7 Software, tools and applications   63

8 The online dimension   75

9 Complementary technologies   85

References   96

Index   99

The authors

David Barber is currently the e-learning Co-ordinator and teaching fellow at Bishop Grosseteste University College and provides advice and training for college staff and students on the use of learning technologies. Active in a number of regional and national groups, David is interested in the promotion of ICT for teaching and research in all educational sectors.

Linda Cooper is a Senior Lecturer on the BA Honours degree programme in Primary education at Bishop Grosseteste University College in Lincoln; she is responsible for delivering the ICT content course. Linda has been a primary school teacher and an ICT co-ordinator. She studied for an MSc in Information Systems and specialised in educational technology focussing on how the use of ICT can enhance teaching and learning in a classroom environment. She has become increasingly interested in interactive whiteboards and their benefits.

Graham Meeson is a Senior Lecturer in Education Studies at Bishop Grosseteste University College, Lincoln and a former Deputy Head Teacher. He has worked on a variety of courses including ITT and Foundation degree programmes focussing on the area of ICT. In the past Graham has acted in a consultancy capacity for his local LEA. He is currently a school governor and has been fascinated by the introduction of interactive whiteboards witnessed in this role and while visiting students in schools.

David Barber
Linda Cooper
Graham Meeson

Introduction

This book is intended for trainee and newly qualified teachers. It explores issues surrounding the installation, operation and application of interactive whiteboards in the primary and early years classroom. Throughout this book the technology will be referred to by the abbreviation IWB. This is a common abbreviation, although you may encounter the alternative, IAW, in other contexts.

The authors of this book are all involved in teacher training and hope that you will find considerable food for thought in the following chapters. We have tried to make the book as practical as possible and it contains numerous classroom stories detailing real-life experiences of teachers and trainees. You will not find many ready-made resources, but there are references to numerous sources where these can be obtained. The main priority has been to equip you with the essential skills required to use an IWB confidently and for the effective creation and evaluation of engaging teaching materials.

Readers will find that two main IWB products are given particular attention. These are the Promethean ACTIVboard™ and the SMART Board™ products. Sections that are of particular relevance to specific models are signalled in the text. However, it is recommended that you read the whole book as discussions of specific products can raise issues of general relevance. Also, to prevent unnecessary repetition, features that are offered by both IWBs may be described more completely for one product than in the description of another. In addition, you should not confine yourself to an understanding of a single product, as you will inevitably be called upon to use both, or others, at some point in your teaching.

1
Technical introduction

By the end of this chapter you should:

- have a clear picture of how IWBs, computers and data projectors work together;
- understand how these devices are connected to one another;
- be aware of potential pitfalls and know how to respond to common problems;
- be able to supervise the effective installation of these devices in a classroom;
- understand the set-up process for both SMART™ and ACTIV boards™.

Professional Standards for QTS

This chapter addresses the following Professional Standards for QTS:

Q8, Q30

Introduction

Potential users often look at an interactive whiteboard as if it were a technical challenge, when it is more accurate to say that the technical hurdle is really just a preliminary to something far more important. The real challenge is the conception and delivery of useful and engaging teaching resources, and much of what figures in future chapters of this book relates to this. However, it is worth providing some technical background right away, for this can serve to dispel any lingering anxieties about using the technology and promotes effective use. It is also, despite everything that has been said so far, useful to have a basic technical understanding of the system so that you can act appropriately when things go wrong.

I have referred to the IWB as a system rather than a device and this is important because we cannot really talk about an IWB without considering two other pieces of equipment. In addition to the IWB itself, you must have a computer, where most of the work takes place, and a data projector, which effectively produces everything you can see. You will certainly have seen a data projector in action and have probably already acquired a broad understanding of how it works. For example, you can doubtless appreciate that a teacher who is able to project an image of what is taking place on their computer is freed from the stricture of 17" (inch) monitor and can share a PowerPoint presentation with a large audience.

Installation

An interactive whiteboard provides an ideal surface for an image to be projected on to, but given its dimensions it requires the projector to be installed in a very precise and stable way. It makes sense, therefore, to install the data projector in a permanent location, normally on the ceiling so as to keep it away from prying fingers. However, by doing so one creates two potential problems that need to be resolved.

The first issue is that you are now dependent on a remote control for switching your projector on and adjusting the picture. You must keep it safe and accessible and should keep spare batteries to hand, for you rarely have much in the way of warning before they expire. You must also familiarise yourself with the remote control handset, for it is very likely that you will need to change the way the projector is set up from time to time. Each brand of projector uses a specific handset, but it is possible to make some helpful observations that apply generally.

Remote Control

Every remote control provides you with a means of switching between different ports that are designed to interface with different devices. There is typically a port for 'video', which may be familiar to you and accommodates three 'pins' that are coloured red, yellow and black. There are also two 'RGB' ports and these are probably the most important for readers of this book. RGB stands for 'Red Green Blue', which is reassuring in that it is comfortingly non-technical, but suffers from being disconcertingly meaningless at the same time. To indulge very briefly in technical jargon, RGB ports are for devices that use a colour model of additive primaries, but my main purpose in making this statement is to persuade you just to accept that this is the port to which you connect your computer.

This arrangement enables you to have two devices plugged in simultaneously and to switch between the two without having to fiddle about with cables every time. To display what is playing on one, you would simply press the relevant button on the remote control, much in the same way as you do when you switch from CD to radio tuner on a home music system. The only complicating factor with the projector's remote is that you normally have only one button for RGB and may therefore need to press it more than once in order to toggle between RGB ports one and two.

Screen-menu

Another feature of all remote controls is access to some sort of screen menu and a set of four arrow keys that allow you to navigate it. These can be a bit tiresome to use and every menu is different, but there are some features that you will need to find sooner or later. Firstly, to install your projector on a ceiling you are obliged to turn the thing on its back. It is therefore possible to invert the image and one thing that occasionally surprises the user of a data projector is that everything appears upside down. This is normally the result of mischief or careless installation, but it is easily remedied by selecting the menu option to 'mirror' or 'switch'. Secondly, there are different 'aspects' or image dimensions, similar in nature to the normal and widescreen settings on a television. It is useful to locate these as certain aspects are better for different things. Aspect 16:9, for example, is good for showing long movies; whereas 4:3 most resembles the proportions of a typical computer monitor. Finally, you may need to make adjustments to the precise alignment of the image so it is useful to find out how to move and resize it along the horizontal and vertical planes. A little exploration and experimentation should soon reveal how all of this is achieved.

Importantly, most remote controls have a button labelled 'Blank' and this is a useful feature that is not used enough. This button makes the data projector stop projecting without turning itself off, and this should be used whenever the projected image is not directly contributing to your lesson. A data projector runs at a high temperature and so turning one on and off is time-consuming. The fan remains on long after the device is switched to standby, for example, and the projector cannot be restarted until the cooling process is complete. Having said this, projectors do use lots of power and the bulbs, which are expensive to replace, have a limited life span. You should always switch a projector off when you have finished using it, but if you are not actually referring to the projected image it is useful to be able to blank it out while you direct the attention of your class elsewhere.

The second issue created by placing the projector on the ceiling is that you now have moved it beyond the reach of the cables that normally come with the machine. The only really effective response to this is to run extensions from the projector, through the ceiling and wall cavities or via surface-trunking, to a wall box somewhere within reach of the computer. This is not a process that you need to worry about as this 'hard-wiring' is all part of the installation process. However, you should be aware that if you take a laptop into an unfamiliar classroom or if you are called upon to check connections on your normal system, the computer should be attached to the projector via a wall box. You will recognise this box, because it is about the size of a small box of chocolates and normally has three sets of ports. The first is trapezoid in shape, protrudes from the face of the wall box in a metal casing and has a regular pattern of holes in a normally blue infill. You will find an identical port on the back of your laptop. These are the RGB ports and need to be connected by a VGA cable. You do not need to know what VGA stands for, but try to remember this in case you are called upon to ask for one. For ease of use this cable normally has blue plugs, thereby matching the colour of the socket.

Speakers and headphones

The next port is a single microphone socket, familiar from such things as a personal stereo or MP3 player, and this should be connected to the identical socket on your computer that is either colour-coded lime green or labelled with an icon that resembles a set of headphones. This will ensure that the sounds coming from your computer are played through the speakers if they have been installed as part of the system. If your system has been installed without speakers, you should not connect your computer to this port as the headphones socket will be required for the speakers that come with the computer. The final set of sockets is for connection to audiovisual devices such as VHS and DVD players, which have already been mentioned. Again you will find that the ports are identical to those on the device that you are trying to connect, so you can normally figure out what goes where by careful observation.

Once you have attached these cables you should be able to turn on the computer and projector and see the image of the former emitting from the latter. If the screen is blank or displaying a message such as 'Cannot find video' or 'No connection on RGB2', you should first press the RGB button on your remote handset. Having done this, if the problem is not resolved, you should check the physical connections outlined above, paying particular attention to the RGB ports on the wall and into the back of your computer. If this does not work, you will need to seek help from someone with a screwdriver or, preferably, another data projector, so always try to test the connections before the class begins.

At this stage you would be forgiven for asking why it was necessary to spend in the region of £1,000–£2,000 on an IWB since it is only serving as a good projection surface. However, the distinctive feature of the IWB is that it closes the triangle, by providing a connection back to the computer. This connection is made via a simple USB or serial cable, which effectively achieves two things. In one direction the cable carries instructions from the IWB to the computer, allowing you to interact with the computer software from the board. To provide a simple example, if a teacher were using a PowerPoint presentation in class they could forget the mouse and advance the slide by simply tapping anywhere on the board. This works because the computer interprets a single tap as a single mouse click. In the other direction the cable carries a little power back to the IWB so no separate power cable is required.

Location

Clearly anyone who is in charge of supervising or planning for an installation within a classroom has a job on their hands, for locating this system requires that a number of considerations be taken into account. It is best to start with the board itself and to think about where to put it, given the arrangement of space within the classroom. Then think about the computer and remember it needs to occupy a permanent location near the board. Ideally you want to avoid a situation where the USB cable lies across the floor. The installers can use a short stretch of surface trunking to carry the cable safely to the desired location, but this means you must have already planned where you intend the computer to be when the board is installed. You do not want to locate the computer too close as you will need to keep all approaches to the IWB open and should reserve some space to either side so that you can stand within reach of the board, but out of the way of the projected image.

These choices will effectively determine the location of the data projector and you can then quickly decide on the best location for the wall box, for it needs to be near the computer. Resist the temptation to locate the box low down out of sight as you will need easy access to it from time to time. You may then leave the cabling to people who have a steady hand for soldering. As a general rule, always ask installers to conduct a site survey and ensure that you explain exactly what you want; they will normally be able to accommodate most needs and may even make helpful suggestions based on their experience elsewhere. Installers may also observe problems created by your plan that you did not foresee; for example, the configuration of ceiling lights. By doing this, you also ensure that you get an accurate quotation and will not get any nasty surprises later. It is also likely that the whole installation is likely to go more smoothly and you will not be liable if unforeseen circumstances cause problems later.

As an alternative to installing the projector on the ceiling you may elect to have it suspended from a wall-mounted pole that extends from a location just above the IWB itself. At an extra cost you can also purchase more expensive projectors that can be fixed at the end of much shorter brackets and which are consequentially less obtrusive. You would normally need a specific reason for doing this, however, an exceptionally high or ornate ceiling perhaps. You can also purchase models of IWB that are designed to work on a back-projection system and do not require an external projector. These are bulky and expensive, but are appropriate in some situations. Finally, you can elect to have the IWB mounted on a trolley. This makes for a more flexible teaching space, but experience suggests that boards on trolleys are used less often than those that are mounted permanently. For one thing they require careful alignment with the projector each time it is used. This kind of complication can introduce a serious disincentive to use of the IWB.

Once you have started your computer and projector and assuming all the necessary connections have been made, you should be able to see your normal 'desktop image' and if you touch the surface of the board with your finger (in the case of SMART Boards™) or the stylus (in the case of Promethean ACTIVboards™) you should find you have control of the cursor. You are now ready to go.

Introducing the SMART Board™

SMART Board™ users should see the 'SMART™ Start Centre' on the screen. This takes the form of a series of icons as depicted below. Starting from the top, these icons provide links to the following tools:

- Notebook Application
  - discussed in Chapter 3
- The SMART Recorder™
  - allows you to record your computer activity
- The SMART Player™
  - allows you to replay videos of your recordings
- The SMART Keyboard™
  - an 'on screen' keyboard that can be used to enter text
- The Floating Toolbar
  - a small menu of useful tools that is always visible
- The System Toolbox
  - contains the option to 'orient' the board (see below)
- Help
  - provides help on various topics
- The 'More…' option
  - allows the user to customise the Start Centre

If the Start Centre is not visible you should look for the SMART™ tools icon on your desktop or – if you are using a PC – in your system tray. The system tray is the set of small icons arranged to the left of your desktop clock.

The best place to start here is with the System Toolbox and specifically with the Orient option. While the projected image will normally occupy the largest space on your IWB you will notice that there is often a small amount of black screen space around the outside. Precisely how much depends on how carefully the installers aligned the projector and whether anyone has fiddled with the image size or the aspect since then. The upshot of this is that the computer is not certain exactly where the image is projected and so doesn't know exactly how to interpret contact with the board at any given location. By orienting the screen you confirm the location of nine fixed points within the projected image on the SMART Board's™ surface and thereby achieve an accurate calibration. Once you have confirmed the ninth point the orientation screen will close and you will be able to test the accuracy of this calibration by touching the board, looking carefully to confirm that the mouse pointer is summoned precisely.

The System Toolbox contains other options that are very useful, but you should explore these by referring to the manufacturer's documentation. I say this partly because of the space it would take to discuss them, but also because you are normally not required to use them until you are quite advanced in your understanding of the system and its software. Reference will be made to the important options at appropriate points within this book.

Returning to the Start Centre menu, we shall pass over the first option as this is covered in considerable detail in Chapter 3. Let us just say that this opens the application that allows you to use the IWB in lieu of a static whiteboard and dry-wipe marker. The second two, the SMART Recorder™ and SMART Player™, are related and although studied in the next chapter it is useful to discuss these options briefly here. You will see that the SMART Board™ can be used to control the computer in a similar way to that in which you are accustomed to using a mouse. You will also see that you can use the pens to create annotations on the board and can introduce images, sounds, internet links and multimedia content to create sophisticated and engaging presentations. One of the most interesting features of the IWB is, as its name suggests, the way in which you can make these presentations dynamic and inter-active. However, sometimes it is useful to be able simply to record whole presentations – or parts of them – and simply play them back. The recorder and the player allow you to do this.

If you click the recorder a control will appear that allows you to start, pause and finish record-ing. Click 'Start' and the system will begin to record everything you do. Obviously there is no external camera so you will not figure physically in the recording, but everything you do on the computer will be recorded. When you click 'Stop' the system will automatically save the recording, pausing to allow you to specify a name for the file and a location in which to store it. This file can then be replayed, either in any media player that you may have installed or by clicking on the SMART Player™ icon on the Start Centre. The advantage of the second option is that you are provided with large buttons that can be moved about the screen and which allow you to perform the normal play, pause and rewind operations.

The SMART Keyboard™ option provides the user with an onscreen keyboard that can be used to input text, into an internet search engine for example, or to model keyboard use. Each new version of the software results in a new version of the keyboard for it is problemati-cal and it is the authors' opinion that you are better preparing lessons in such a way that you are not obliged to do any typing, or resort to the physical keyboard when it cannot be avoided. For example, to save typing web addresses into internet browsers, ensure that the sites you want to visit are stored in your list of favourites or bookmarks. If you anticipate using text make sure that this is typed in before the lesson and drag it into play when it is needed – this process and terms like 'dragging' will be explained later.

If you do decide to use the keyboard you will find that it works in a fairly predictable way. You simply tap on the keys to enter letters or to give commands such as 'Enter'. You may find, depending on the version of the software you are using, that the letters you type appear in a text box just above the number keys and are not committed until you click a 'Submit' button. Alternatively, you may find that they are entered straight onto the screen. In each case make sure that the cursor is in the right place – in the right text box on a form, for example, or in the right place within a document – before you start typing. Opening the keyboard can cause the location of your cursor to change so always double check just before typing to avoid confusion.

Below the keyboard you will find the option to activate the Floating Toolbar and once you are more comfortable using the SMART Board™ you may find it useful to do so. The Floating Toolbar contains the most useful drawing and screen-capture tools and 'floats', in the sense that it is never covered by any windows or programs that you might open subsequently. It therefore ensures that these tools are always easily available to you.

You will also find that you can access help via the Start Centre and you should never be afraid to do so, particularly when preparing presentations. Doing so may serve not only to remind you how to perform some task or another, but may reveal better or more efficient ways of achieving specific effects.

Finally you have the '...' or 'More' option, which allows you to customise the start centre. This can be useful as it makes it possible to introduce new tools such as the 'Spotlight' and it is useful to discuss this specific tool in anticipation of future passages which refer to it. The spotlight is useful for focusing attention on a specific part of the screen or concealing others, as it effectively blanks out all but a specifically designated area. By default the spotlight is circular, but you have the option to change its shape in a variety of ways. You can also move the spotlight by touching the board near to the edge but outside the lit-up area, and drawing your finger across the surface to a new location. Drawing your finger across the board from a location somewhere on the circumference of the lit-up area, either towards or away from the centre, will cause the spotlight to shrink or grow in size.

Getting started with a Promethean ACTIVboard™

This IWB does not require a 'Start Centre' in quite the same way as the SMART Board™, for reasons that will become apparent later. The manufacturers of the ACTIVboard™ have taken a different approach, largely focused on the central importance of an electronic stylus. However, in common with the SMART Board™, you do need to orient the device, as the computer cannot know precisely where within the bounds of the board the image is projected. These bounds are marked physically on the board's surface by four white corner guides and a Promethean user initiates the calibration process by tapping the pen nib on a white mark that extends from the bottom left-hand guide.

If this has no effect, tap repeatedly within the region immediately around the spot until the screen changes. Once this happens you will find that you are invited to confirm the location of nine fixed locations on the surface of the board. This is explained in more detail above as it is virtually identical to the orientation process on the SMART Board™. However, once you have completed this operation the calibration screen will disappear and you should find that you are able to summon and control the mouse pointer precisely. Try tapping the board with the pen to confirm this.

You have control of the computer straight away and the board is able to follow your movements as it stays in constant contact with the pen via a sensor in the top right-hand corner. You will find that you do not need to touch the surface of the board in order to control the mouse pointer, but are actually able to summon and guide the mouse pointer by placing the pen nib close to the surface. We shall explore the implications of this in more detail later.

To get the most from the equipment you need to run the ACTIV™ software that you intend to use. In this book it is assumed that you are using the ACTIVprimary™ software, but the difference between this and the ACTIVstudio™ package is largely one of presentation. This is not to say that the differences are not significant, for they are of the greatest importance in terms of how the software is used, and the ACTIVprimary™ software makes the board useable by primary age children. However, an ACTIVstudio™ user should be able to apply much of what is said in future chapters because the same tools are available to them, just in a very different interface.

Once you load the ACTIVprimary™ software you will see that it completely obscures your desktop view, but you can conceal the interface by clicking the button on the side toolbar that resembles a flat-screen computer monitor. This reveals the desktop once more and puts the main tools onto a handy, but much smaller, Floating Toolbar. By 'floating' I mean that this toolbar will never be obscured by any other windows or any other applications that you open subsequently. Clicking the large button in the top right-hand corner will invoke the main software interface once more.

 This reveals the desktop

 This restores the software interface

By exploring this Floating Toolbar or the extended toolbars within the ACTIVprimary™ interface you will discover all the facilities described in the section above on the SMART Board™. The illustrations below indicate the icons for these tools and how to find them.

 If you click on this button, which is located in the top section of the right-hand tool bar, you will cause a selection of tools to be displayed along the bottom of the screen.

 If you select this tool you will invoke the Spotlight tool. Upon clicking the button you will be offered the option of an elliptical or rectangular spotlight which will then follow the pen as it moves across the surface of the board. If you press the pen nib against the surface of the board and move it with the nib depressed, you will cause the spotlight to change dimensions.

 If you select this tool you will activate the Recorder, which causes a small panel of controls including record, play, pause and rewind. When you click 'Record' the system begins to record everything you do. (Obviously you are not yourself recorded, but everything you do – your movement of the mouse-pointer, for example, or opening windows and navigating the internet – is.)

In addition to this you may also be interested in one tool that was introduced to users of the SMART Board™ and which has not been discussed for the ACTIVboard™ solution. This is the on-screen keyboard and you can refer above for a brief discussion of how this can be used, for the same general considerations apply. To access the ACTIVprimary™ keyboard you must close the interface so that you can see the Floating Toolbar. The button you need is located in the bottom right-hand corner and very vaguely resembles a keyboard.

Conclusion

People tend to say of SMART Boards™ that they are intuitive and tactile, promoting easy use by both teachers and children. If you have referred to a SMART Board™ while reading this chapter it is very likely that you will have already found it difficult to resist picking up the pens and using them on the surface of the board. You may have encountered a few unexpected events, such as annotations disappearing, but intuition will very probably already have allowed you to start giving your computer simple instructions by tapping or stroking the screen and to start drawing over the Windows environment using the pens.

Owners of ACTIVboards™ may feel somewhat differently at this stage. At this point you will probably feel a little daunted about wielding the pen and will already recognise that the software is relatively complex. However, you may have begun to start exploring some of the other options in the tools menu and are probably quite impressed with the attractive and child-friendly interface. If you have, you will already have appreciated the powerful features offered by the ACTIVprimary™ software and although we will see that many have equivalents within parts of the SMART™ software that we have not encountered yet, many users like the breadth and sophistication of the built-in tools available on the ACTIVboard™.

PRACTICAL TASK PRACTICAL TASK **PRACTICAL TASK** PRACTICAL TASK **PRACTICAL TASK**

Orient your board and then attempt to create a video of the orientation process. To do so:

- Locate the button for the recorder tool and press it.
- Start the recorder.
- Initiate the orientation process and orient the board.
- Once you have completed that task, test the calibration by summoning the mouse pointer to various locations on the screen with your finger or the ACTIVstylus™.
- Stop the recorder.
- Play back your video using the IWB's movie player.

A SUMMARY OF KEY POINTS

After reading of this chapter you should be aware of the following points:

> the way that the computer, data projector and IWB work together;
> issues relating to the installation of these devices;
> issues relating to the integration of these devices into a working system and how to respond to the most commonly-encountered problems;
> how to initiate a whiteboard session and how to orient the board in preparation for its use in the classroom.

2
Getting started

By the end of this chapter you should:

- understand the IWB and its various modes of operation;
- use pens and other supporting hardware;
- work with the software that comes with your whiteboard.

Professional Standards for QTS

This chapter addresses the following Professional Standards for QTS:

Q8, Q9, Q16, Q25a

Introduction

You will not have to look very hard to find cases where IWB technology has been adopted with confidence and a genuine desire to enhance teaching and learning. However, you will also encounter examples of IWB use that are tentative and lack confidence. In some cases fear or suspicion of the technology can distract the user from more important pedagogical issues. This chapter aims to ensure that you operate the technology with assurance and can focus on lesson content and learning outcomes, unhampered by technical difficulties.

As you will have already realised, there are a number of IWB manufacturers and you may well come across several different products in your teaching. However, each solution represents a response to identical problems and offers a similar range of functionality. For example, every model must allow the user to work within the kind of computer software environments that we are all familiar with, such as MS Windows or Mac OS. Therefore, although it highlights the main differences between the market leaders and discusses the different challenges associated with their product, this chapter also focuses on the core functions common to all IWBs and on skills that are generally applicable.

This approach is important and you should avoid becoming exclusively attached to one kind of IWB. As with other aspects of your experience in school, the wider exposure you have to different approaches, the greater your eventual versatility as a teacher.

Modes and modality

Before beginning to describe IWBs it is worthwhile spending some time considering the notion of modes and modality.

A modal device is one that can assume different states and behave differently according to which state or mode it is currently in. If you consider the humble computer mouse, you are aware that it performs a surprisingly wide range of functions, given its apparent simplicity. It allows you to move the 'pointer' across two dimensions and is typically used to browse menus, select content, activate hyperlinks, check boxes, set radio buttons, move sliders, and so on. In certain software packages the mouse may be used to simulate the role of a paintbrush, eraser or drawing tool; in others you can use it to shoot rubber ducks, save colonies of lemmings, judge a professional golfer's backswing and even realise the ballistic aspirations of heavily armed worms.

Of course it is the software that does most of the work, for it allows the simple tools afforded by the mouse to assume a variety of roles. This is particularly clear in drawing programs, where a toolbar allows the user effectively to transform the mouse into a different kind of drawing tool with a single click. One button turns your mouse into a facility for creating freehand doodles; another allows you to draw rectangles or circles. However, many software applications are designed so that we are not conscious of modes – or at least we do not need to be.

Put briefly, modes allow designers to make simple tools perform a wide variety of functions. This concept is invaluable for the designers of an IWB, for their challenge is to provide the user with a way of controlling the computer without a mouse or a keyboard and to provide a facility equivalent to a static whiteboard. What is more, since the user needs to work in front of an audience, they are less able to handle the distractions of a complex input device. The approach adopted by most IWB products, therefore, is to create a simple input device, something resembling a pen, which behaves like a mouse in one mode and like a dry-wipe marker in another. As we shall see, this is a poor summary of a system that exceeds both the mouse and the dry-wipe marker in terms of classroom functionality. However, it is a good place to start.

Mouse mode

Mouse mode enables you to control the computer using your finger or some other pointing device. Once everything is turned on and the projector and IWB are connected to the computer, you will see an image of whatever is currently displayed on the computer screen projected onto the IWB. At this stage the board itself will be in 'mouse mode'; it is set up to interpret any interaction by you as an attempt to give instructions to the computer.

SMART Board™

If you are using a SMART Board™ you can simply touch the screen with your finger and you will notice that by doing so you summon the mouse pointer to that location. If you tap on an area of the screen that is occupied by an icon, the system responds as though a single mouse click had occurred, in this case by highlighting the designated icon. Two short taps in quick succession are treated as a double click and open the document or the shortcut represented by that icon. If you place your finger on the screen and draw it along the surface to another location you are performing the equivalent of a 'click and drag' operation (see Practical Task – Part 1). You are, to put it simply, using the IWB as though it were a big, flat mouse.

Using a Promethean ACTIVboard™

To perform the same functions on a Promethean ACTIVboard™ you would first load the ACTIVstudio™ software and then use the stylus to touch the board and would imitate mouse clicks by tapping the board with the 'nib', which can 'click' like a button. As with the SMART Board™ you tap once for a single click and twice for a double click. Pressing the button on the body of the pen while the nib is touching the board is equivalent to a double click, while drawing the nib across the board without clicking either the button or the nib allows other operations such as moving content around the screen or manipulating tools such as spot-lights and blinds.

Once you have become comfortable manipulating the pen, you will realise that the same principles that apply to the SMART Board™ apply here too. Clicks and double clicks are almost exactly the same, while clicking and dragging is just a question of acquiring the sub-tleness of touch to stroke the pen across the board without clicking the nib. You will find that actual contact is not required for this kind of action, as the board is able to detect the pen when it is very close to the surface.

PRACTICAL TASK PRACTICAL TASK **PRACTICAL TASK** PRACTICAL TASK **PRACTICAL TASK**

Pointing, clicking and dragging

You have just encountered the three principal mouse operations and seen how they are performed on an IWB. It is a good idea to start practising them as soon as possible, for developing confidence at this basic level of operation is the foundation stone of all effective practice. Try using the whiteboard to perform the following basic tasks.

Close all applications on your computer so you are just looking at your desktop. Use simple taps to navigate your file directory and open two folders which contain documents or shortcuts.

1 Define a space: press on the IWB and then move your finger or pen over the board without breaking contact with the surface (a 'stroke'). This will define a rectangular space and selects anything that is partly or wholly encompassed within it. Observe that this rectangle appears as a dotted outline on the screen until you remove your finger from the board.
2 Select multiple documents in one folder by defining a space around them (as in 1 above).
3 Move the group by touching the screen at the location of one of the selected documents and drag them into the other folder by running your finger or pen across the surface of the board, removing your finger only once you are pointing at the destination folder.
4 Tap (select) and drag (stroke) all the documents back again, one by one. On a mouse the initial tap or click and subsequent drag would normally be a single operation. However, on an IWB it is sometimes more reliable to tap to select and then drag.

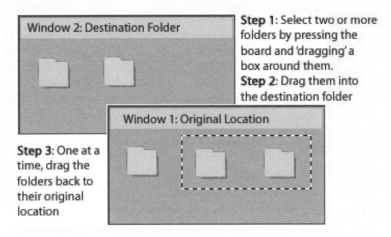

Figure 2.1. Controlling the computer with an IWB

You should note that defining a region of space and moving an object are similar processes. If your initial point of contact coincides with a selected object (e.g. an icon), that object will follow the direction of any subsequent stroke. Otherwise, the same gesture defines a region. When you remove your finger from the board, the computer will attempt to leave the object that you have been dragging at that point. If it is not able to do so for any reason, it will simply return the object to its original location. We will see much more of this when we look at the IWB software.

Moving objects confidently in this way is absolutely central to SMART Board™ use. You may find that positioning yourself with your back to the board and using the nail of your finger rather than the pad helps. This means you are facing the class and the nail provides a smoother, more dependable contact.

One way of reliably dragging on a Promethean board is to angle the pen so that the nib-end of the handle's casing is touching the board, so that the nib is held very close to or just touching the surface. With a little practice, what appears to be a highly dextrous manoeuvre can be performed with virtually no thought at all.

Context menus

Context menus are extremely important for IWB use. On a PC a single click on the right mouse button evokes a menu that contains options appropriate to the location of the mouse pointer when the click was made. On a Macintosh, the same effect can be achieved by holding down the 'Ctrl' key and clicking the single mouse button. These are called 'context menus' or 'shortcut menus'. For example, 'right-click' on a block of selected (highlighted) text within a word-processing application and you will call up a menu including options appropriate to that context – Cut, Copy and Delete for example. Right-click on empty desktop space, on the other hand, and you get options to customise display properties and to refresh the desktop. The advantage of this facility when using an IWB is that right-clicks make menu options available in more accessible locations, saving unnecessary stretching for toolbars and menus.

SMART Board™

The shelf that contains the pens and the eraser is also home to two buttons. One is identified by a mouse icon, the other by a keyboard icon. If you click the 'mouse' button you cause the SMART Board™ to go into a temporary state that we might refer to as 'right-click mode'. On the next occasion that you touch the screen with your finger, the system will respond as though a right mouse button click had just occurred. At this point the system returns to its normal state and any subsequent taps on the surface of the screen will be interpreted as though they were 'left-clicks'. The other button summons a 'screen keyboard', an image of a keyboard with keypad buttons that you can tap. This can be used to model keyboard use or to input information into forms.

Promethean

A similar menu of core functions can be summoned at any time and at any location by placing the pen close the surface of the board and clicking the side button.

Once you have mastered these mouse operations you are ready to perform a surprising range of activities in the classroom. Many software applications and online activities can be incorporated into lessons in a seamless and transparent way. The IWB allows you to demonstrate and model activities and processes much more clearly than if the computer needed to be operated using a mouse and keyboard. Perhaps most significantly it allows you to incorporate internet resources and the communication tools available on the World Wide Web into group teaching much more effectively. You might also use the IWB to explain or even work through learning objects that you have created in applications like MSWord or Excel. Remember, anything that you can do with a mouse can be done directly onto an IWB.

Drawing mode

All IWBs provide facilities which allow you to 'draw' by using a pen or your finger to write or to describe lines, shapes and dots on the board itself. This leaves no physical trace, but the board senses the movement of your pen or your finger and translates this movement into signals that it sends to the computer. The computer processes these signals, translates them back into lines, dots, words, and so on and draws them over the image it is currently displaying. This image is fed back through the projector so you appear to be drawing directly onto the board. Typically you will also be able to erase annotations and drawings, either wholesale or selectively.

SMART Boards™ provide plastic pens and an eraser that sit in a tray that runs along the bottom of the board. These provide a handy means of drawing on the board and have soft contact points that are designed for the purpose. However, they are just plastic instruments and have no complex electronic components. Promethean boards, on the other hand, depend on a special pen-like device that actively communicates with a copper mesh that is buried in the solid melamine body of the board itself.

The pen on a Promethean board is a versatile tool. Used in conjunction with the Floating Toolbar, the pen can be made to work in a variety of ways. We have seen that it can function as a mouse, but it can also be used as a conventional pen, in lieu of a dry-wipe marker or as a means of controlling features such as spotlights and blinds or implementing other tools. How the pen behaves depends upon which mode is selected on the ACTIVprimary™ toolbar (the ACTIVprimary™ software is part of the ACTIVstudio™ package and is the aspect of the software that you interact with).

Drawing – the SMART Board™ solution

When using a SMART Board™, picking up any of the equipment on the bottom shelf causes the device to change mode. A light above the empty tray indicates this and while any of the lights are lit the user can draw by applying the pen to the surface of the board in exactly the same way as they would use a dry-wipe marker. Since the pen is just a 'dumb' piece of plastic, the user could remove the pen from its tray and draw or write with their finger instead.

This gives the SMART Board™ two highly positive attributes. Firstly, changing between 'mouse mode' and 'drawing mode' is made very simple and intuitive: you pick up a pen to draw and return it to its tray when you want to change back. The key advantage of this is that you do not even need to think consciously about changing mode. Secondly, since you can choose to interact with the board using your hand, the membrane has a tactile quality that other IWBs lack. From the point of view of classroom applications, it can be highly useful for the teacher to control the mode by picking up or replacing the pen in its tray, but at the same time allow the children to interact with the board using their fingers.

This approach does have some drawbacks. You must ensure that you only touch the surface of the SMART Board™ with the pen or with the part of your body you intended. If the board senses two simultaneous points of contact it will attempt to draw a line connecting them. This will interrupt what you are doing and mess up the end result, so some care must be taken in regulating the ways in which groups of children use the board.

Secondly, annotations that are made on SMART Boards™ are unstable, unless they are done in conjunction with a particular piece of software that we will examine in much more detail later. If a user adds annotations over a Windows application, for example, and then reverts to mouse mode, they will lose those annotations upon their next contact with the board. This is by no means as significant as it first appears, as we shall soon see that there are relatively few occasions when one needs to make stable annotations over normal Windows applications. However, it is another pitfall that can trip up an inexperienced user or someone who is accustomed to a Promethean board. It is also an important consideration to bear in mind when using the board with groups of children.

Drawing – the Promethean solution

In order to do anything interactive on the Promethean ACTIVboard™, the ACTIVstudio™ software must be loaded first. This ensures that the pen and the board communicate effectively and provides a toolbar that allows the user to change between mouse and drawing mode and to select from a range of tools. The ACTIVprimary™ toolbar consists of child-friendly blocks of buttons, each with its own icon. These effectively frame the normal image of your computer desktop and any windows that you have opened from it. This means you always have direct access to important tools and can make a wide range of annotations, including shapes and straight lines, over everything that takes place within a Windows environment.

To start drawing, the user taps the 'Freehand Drawing' button or any one of the built-in annotation tools with the pen. These annotation tools include shapes, lines, arrows, grids and more. By doing so the user moves the system into 'Annotation mode' and an 'Annotate over Windows' button, labelled with an arrowhead, will automatically change its appearance as though it has been and remains depressed. Regardless of which form of drawing you initially selected, you can return to mouse mode at any time by clicking the 'Annotate over Windows' button, effectively cancelling your last click.

This approach has advantages. Because the ACTIVstudio™ software is constantly running in the background, annotations made over the top of Windows applications are stable and will persist until deleted. The use of the pen also means that the Promethean board allows users to write on the board in a much more natural fashion. For example, they can rest the heel of their hand on the surface of the board while writing or drawing and no one else can interfere with what the holder of the pen is doing.

However, users, particularly children, do need to acclimatise to using the pen and the process of moving between modes is also potentially problematic, particularly for the inexperienced user or for someone who is accustomed to using a SMART Board™. The process is not intuitive and depends on the user remembering which mode they are in. In this situation you may well try to open a file or follow a link, but instead of controlling the computer as though the IWB were a mouse, you end up drawing dots on the screen as though it were a static whiteboard. It is often difficult, especially when you are close up, to observe what is happening. Inevitably you conclude that the computer is at fault, but from a distance the reality of the situation is plain to see. It is exactly this kind of experience that can cause embarrassment and undermine confidence in using the technology.

Drawing over windows on IWBs

If you are using a Promethean board it is a good idea to become familiar with the floating toolbar as quickly as possible. In particular, you should try to habituate yourself to the process of changing between modes. Many of the menu buttons on the Floating Toolbar are what are generally referred to as radio buttons, which is to say they invoke a tool or create an effect that remains active until another tool or function is selected. Others, such as the button for the spotlight, invoke a specialised tool that is closed by another means, normally an on-screen button or menu. The 'Annotate over Windows' mode, however, is an example of a button that works like a light switch. The same button, in other words, is pressed in order to move between two different states or modes, in this case annotation mode and mouse mode. Clicking menu buttons of this kind is often referred to as toggling.

PRACTICAL TASK PRACTICAL TASK **PRACTICAL TASK** PRACTICAL TASK **PRACTICAL TASK**

Moving between modes and drawing
Use your finger (SMART Board™) or the stylus provided (Promethean) to open a web browser (if you have an internet connection) or a simple document (if you haven't).

- Move into drawing mode and, if you are using a Promethean board, practise using the freehand drawing button, or any of the other annotation tools to highlight text or create connections between elements within the document. If you are using a SMART Board™, do the same thing by removing a pen from its tray and then using it or your finger to draw on the board.
- Experiment with using different colours and try erasing as well as creating annotations.
- Periodically, move back into mouse mode, by toggling the 'Annotate over Windows' button, and then either navigate to a different web page or open a different document.
- Try to think analytically about what you are doing and to relate aspects of your experience to the advantages and drawbacks of the device you are using. However, remember that at this stage you have only been introduced to the software that comes with each system and so the drawbacks of both systems will seem greater than they really are.

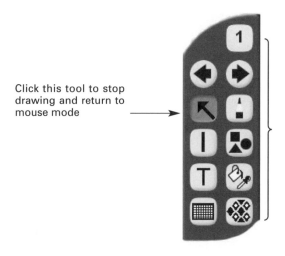

Click this tool to stop drawing and return to mouse mode

These tools allow you to annotate, draw lines and shapes and insert writing or backgrounds

Figure 2.2. Part of the ACTIVprimary™ toolbar

It is very important that you start to think critically about how and in what circumstances the IWB adds real value to your teaching. It is not the case that the whiteboard is appropriate in every situation, and learning how to become a discriminating user is the single most important skill that you need to develop in relation to this technology.

CLASSROOM STORY **CLASSROOM** STORY CLASSROOM STORY **CLASSROOM STORY**

Hannah is a first-year QTS trainee. She has been placed in a Year 5 class and is beginning to become familiar with the IWB in her classroom. The focus of the lesson involves making annotations on a piece of text for redrafting. She is modelling the activity on the whiteboard for the children.

Hannah begins by opening a Word file, using mouse mode. This is done by 'double-tapping' the folder and file icons on the projected image of her desktop. This opens a Word version of a story opening that she has drafted for the lesson. The children read this out aloud with her. Once they have completed reading the text they begin to identify areas for redrafting. This is done in a number of stages:

- Hannah underlines areas that could be redrafted in red.
- She then revises the redrafting symbols used within the school in green.
- She invites the children to come and write on the IWB.
- Finally, Hannah prints out this annotated piece of writing. This printout is photocopied, placed on the children's tables and used as a model to assist their work (we will look at how this is achieved in the next chapter).

REFLECTIVE TASK
REFLECTIVE TASK

Identify three ways that the IWB supports you as a teacher and three ways in which it might improve the experience of the children in your care. For each item in your list try to provide some context in terms of a specific classroom activity and consider how access to the technology would influence how you structure and develop that activity.

You should not think about the particular model that you have access to, but rather focus on the generic advantages of being able to control your computer directly through the board and to annotate over the top of the projected image.

You may find that this is quite hard to do, for we have hardly glanced at the software that really unleashes the potential of this technology. However, this will provide a useful basis for the reflective tasks in future chapters.

A SUMMARY OF **KEY POINTS**

As a result of reading this chapter you should now be able to:

> change modes;
> operate the computer using the IWB interface;
> click and drag items on the whiteboard;
> draw using pen tools.

Useful websites

At this stage you should simply visit the websites of the two products discussed here:

www.prometheanworld.com/uk/
www.smarttech.com/

3
Software

By the end of this chapter you should:

- understand the importance of software to IWB use;
- be familiar with the SMART Notebook™ and ACTIVprimary™ applications;
- understand how to create text and insert graphics;
- understand how to import content from the internet and elsewhere;
- be comfortable moving, resizing and manipulating components within a presentation;
- be comfortable working with presentations using several slides.

Professional Standards for QTS

This chapter addresses the following Professional Standards for QTS:

Q4, Q7, Q8, Q16, Q17, Q23, Q25a

Introduction

An IWB provides a means of interacting with a computer and can take the place of a whiteboard and dry-wipe marker. This requires two broad types of software. There is the software that trundles along in the background and just keeps the different components in the system talking to each other. This allows you to perform all the tasks discussed in the previous chapter. Then there is the more familiar kind of software, the computer applications that allow you to design and deliver presentations and activities. This is the focus of the present chapter.

The ability to create presentations in an electronic format means that classroom resources can be created on a computer and saved to a portable disk or memory stick. The SMART Notebook™ and the ACTIVprimary™ software can be installed on most computers, even if they are not connected to an IWB, and they can then be controlled by a mouse. If you intend to use an IWB on a regular basis it is useful to obtain a copy of the software that you intend to use and install it on a computer that you have regular access to. This will allow you to get the most from your equipment as you can prepare resources in a relatively comfortable environment.

Both software packages allow you compose presentations from text, images, animations, free-hand annotations, drawings, video clips and sound files. What is more, content can typically be split across several slides, allowing a user to develop a resource that involves several discrete parts, much like the slides in a PowerPoint presentation. However, unlike the content of a PowerPoint presentation, anything in an IWB presentation can be resized, rotated and moved about the screen or even between screens. You are also able to add more content in a seamless fashion as you go, building on the materials you have prepared as the lesson progresses.

This content could come from a variety of sources and anything you create in other computer programs and much of what you discover on the internet can be copied and pasted in to your growing resource. The World Wide Web is a particularly fecund source, although you must always consider the implications of copyright and intellectual property rights. There is a large volume of materials that are freely available for use in teaching and requests to use restricted content for educational purposes are often very well received. Nevertheless, you must obtain written permission when it is not expressly provided and must respect any refusal. It can be safer and less time consuming to create a hyperlink to internet content and all IWB software packages provide a means of doing so (more is said on this subject later).

Finally, for this generic summary, IWB software packages allow the user to take a 'snapshot' of what they are doing at any stage, creating an image file of either the whole projected image or a region of the screen that is defined by the user themselves. This serves as an excellent record of learning or teaching and can easily be saved to disk, printed out or distributed to the class or to anyone else via email. This simple facility is very powerful and apart from anything else means that a teacher can recycle any teaching resources they create without losing all record of what a class has done with them.

SMART Notebook™

In common with many applications, the Notebook application opens to reveal a work space or 'content area' and a series of menus and toolbars. In addition to this a side panel on the right contains a scaled-down image (or 'thumbnail') of the main content area. Initially you will see one blank thumbnail, but this will change and will be joined by others as your presentation grows. Ultimately you will be able to jump to any slide in your presentation by tapping on its thumbnail.

This panel is labelled 'Slide Sorter' and when you are not using it will often 'roll up', giving over more screen space to the content area. To open the slide sorter again just click on the label or 'tab' or, if you are currently dragging something, slide your finger across the board's surface to the tab and pause there until the panel opens. You will also see two other tabs: one called 'Gallery' and the other called 'Attachments'. The first contains a library of handy images and other kinds of content that can be dragged into your presentation. The second allows you to add materials of your own, effectively expanding your library of reusable resources. To access either of these simply tap on those labels and the relevant panel will appear in place of the slide sorter.

The tools

Returning our attention to the bars across the top, we find a menu bar that contains some familiar and some less familiar options. These menus provide access to all the tools and settings you need, but the most important menu options, including all those that are peculiar to the Notebook software, are represented in the toolbar that resides immediately below. We shall now look at this more closely.

Some of these icons should be familiar to you from other applications and the ones below allow you to perform rudimentary processes.

   Creating, opening and saving documents

   Pasting content (that has been copied from elsewhere)

   Zoom in on an area of the screen

   Undo or redo things that you have done

It should be emphasised at this point that copying and pasting, though a simple and probably familiar operation, is of great importance for it allows you to import content that has been created in a wide variety of popular applications and the internet. You are not, in other words, restricted to moving content within an application, but can do so between applications as well.

Here are six icons that are more or less unique to the notepad application.

The first two allow you to navigate sequentially, backwards and forwards, through a series of slides. There is also a Blind tool that causes an opaque grey overlay to appear on top of the content area. This has handles on each side, which can be 'grabbed' – i.e. tapped on – and dragged towards the centre, thereby revealing the content behind in stages. The next button causes the content area to be displayed across the whole area of the screen, while the last activates the Snapshot tool.

If you click the Snapshot button a small dialogue box will appear, offering three options. The first option allows you to specify a region of the screen by clicking and dragging; the next selects the whole screen; and the third selects only the active window. Once you have chosen, the system greys out the areas it intends to copy and if this is confirmed (tap the camera icon in the centre of the greyed-out region) its contents are copied and added to your current presentation as a new slide. You may then access this slide like any other, but you will notice that you cannot manipulate its contents in any way; it is simply a static snapshot of whatever was being displayed at the time.

The remaining icons or buttons on the toolbar refer to tools from the drawing menu and these are exploded in Figure 3.1. From here you can choose a variety of colours and styles for freehand drawing. Other buttons allow you to draw straight lines with various kinds of arrow-heads and other terminations and you can create basic shapes such as stars, rectangles and oblongs. You will also find buttons that allow you to format typed text and to set a range of properties such as colour, line thickness and opacity.

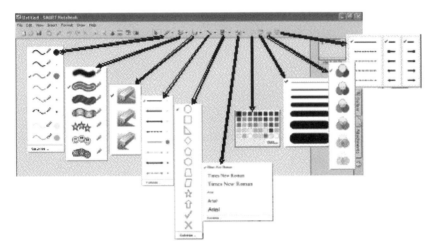

Figure 3.1. Notebook toolbar items (SMART Board™ Interactive Whiteboard screenshots courtesy of SMART Technologies Inc.™ All rights reserved.)

You tend to use this toolbar more often when creating presentations, when you may not have access to the IWB and its pen tools. However, you may well use these tools during a presentation too – in order to create shapes or arrows, for example. In either case, using the tools on this toolbar bypasses the normal process of using the pen tray to shift into drawing mode and as a consequence you cannot return to mouse mode in the normal way. You therefore need a quick and simple way of moving the system back into mouse mode. You can do this by clicking the Selector button, which is depicted below:

     Selector button

Adding content

We have so far seen several ways of adding content. You can use the toolbars described above to create simple graphics or typed text and you can use basic cut-and-paste operations to introduce content from elsewhere. In addition you can use the pen tools to create annotations and freehand drawings simply by picking up a pen and drawing within the content area of the screen and you can drag pre-prepared graphics and flash tools from the gallery.

Every time you introduce a new piece of content the system defines it as a separate 'object', which means that you can continue to select it and manipulate it separately from everything else. To select an object you simply tap on it, causing a blue, rectangular box to appear around it. This 'bounding box' has two 'handles': a green circle that extends from the top edge of the bounding box, and a white circle that is located at the bottom right-hand corner.

A selected object can be moved within the content area or into any other slide, by dragging the item to a new location or onto one of the thumbnails in the slide sorter. You can also click and drag the white circle, either towards or away from the centre of the object, to increase its size, or rotate it by dragging the green circle in one or another direction.

A consequence of this approach is that you must try to anticipate what components of your presentation need to be manipulated independently of one another. This is particularly true when you are writing or drawing freehand, for in this case you need to consciously define separate objects. For example, if you were assembling a list of names you could define each name as a separate object and then sort or group them freely in later stages of the activity. The IWB is not good at making this sort of judgement, but you can tell the system when you have completed an object by returning the pen to its tray. In our example we would do so after writing each name.

Manipulating content

In addition to moving things about, it is also possible to edit the properties of discrete objects independently of one another. If you click on any object you will see that, in addition to the green and white handles referred to above, there is also a little box with a downward-pointing arrowhead located in the top right-hand corner. If you click on this you will see a pop-up menu appear, as illustrated in Figure 3.2.

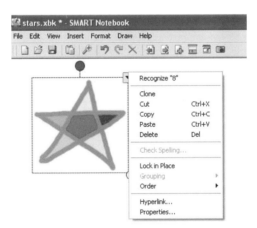

Figure 3.2. Content manipulation menu (SMART Board™ Interactive Whiteboard photographs courtesy of SMART Technologies Inc™. All rights reserved.)

This menu gives you access to more or less all the tools that apply to manipulating screen objects. The object depicted in this illustration is not text, but the system is nevertheless attempting to provide a reasonable translation. If one were to tap on 'Recognise "8"' it would convert the whole thing into an editable piece of typed text, the character 8 in this case. As you can probably already appreciate, converting words and even whole sentences from freehand annotations into typed text is a quick process. What is more, the system will often volunteer several different possible interpretations of what you have written – so it is pretty reliable.

The next set of options should be familiar, although 'Clone', which is equivalent to the whole cut-and-paste operation, may not be. Click on this option and a copy of your selected object will appear, slightly overlapping the original. This can then be dragged to any location on or between screens.

Below this you have an option to check spelling and in Figure 3.2 this is greyed out, as it would not be applicable until you had converted the object into typed text.

Next we come to three options that are very important for resource design: 'Lock in place', 'Grouping' and 'Order'. If you click on 'Lock in place' you will, as the term implies, lock the selected object so that it cannot be moved, resized or manipulated in any way. Any subsequent tap on this object will evoke a single option to 'Unlock'. This is very useful in designing resources because you can lock components in a template that you don't want to move inadvertently. For example, the rings in a Venn diagram could be locked since you wouldn't want to accidentally move them in the process of populating the various sections created by their intersection.

In order for the Grouping option to have any effect you must either have more than one object or an already grouped set of objects selected. Clicking this option would allow you to join several objects into one – lots of separate words into one sentence, for example – or split up an existing group. Grouping is often used for convenience. Say you had grouped a collection of boys' names from a pool of mixed examples, you might then choose to group them so that you can move or resize them in one operation. However, grouping can be used to great effect in prepared presentations, allowing you to link different components within a presentation so that moving one object moves another, revealing or concealing another area of the screen perhaps. To select two objects simultaneously you may either click and drag a selection box (i.e. tap on empty space and drag) around the two objects you want to group or hold down the 'Ctrl' key on your keyboard and click each object separately.

Tap on 'Order' and you will be provided with several options that affect the level or layer that the object is assigned to. This will influence whether it conceals or is concealed by other objects at a given location. You may move your object straight to the top or bottom layer ('Send to back' and 'Bring to front') or move one layer in either direction ('Send backward' and 'Bring forward'). Organising content across layers is important and it is always a good idea to rehearse an activity to check that the ordering of the various objects is as effective as it can be. Be warned that selecting an object when it is covered by another at a given location can be problematical.

Finally, you have two further options, 'Hyperlink' and 'Properties'. Click on 'Hyperlink' and you will be confronted with a dialogue box that invites you to supply a web address. From this point on, this object will have a small symbol attached to it. Any tap on that object from then on will activate the hyperlink and the web page you specified will appear in a new window. This is a powerful way of increasing the scope of your presentation and can help you avoid all kinds of copyright and intellectual property issues.

If you click on 'Properties' you will find that a dialogue box appears containing all the options on the toolbar. This may seem redundant, but given that you need to stretch every time you reach for the toolbar you will find this dialogue box a real boon when working in a classroom situation. Apart from anything else this dialogue box contains an image of the object that changes as you fiddle with the properties, effectively allowing you to preview the impact of the changes you are making before you click 'OK' and commit them to your presentation.

ACTIVstudio™

The ACTIVprimary™ software package is a version of the ACTIVstudio™ software that is appropriate for use with young children, having controls that are incorporated into a child-friendly interface. A panel located along the bottom of the screen provides access to 'tool-trays' that children would typically use; while another, running up the right-hand side, contains what are characterised as teachers' tools. This view of the system is called the flipchart view (see Figure 3.3), but the user can conceal the flipchart at any time, revealing the normal Windows desktop. Having done this the user is then able to control the computer via the stylus and may access a range of annotation tools from a less obtrusive, Floating Toolbar.

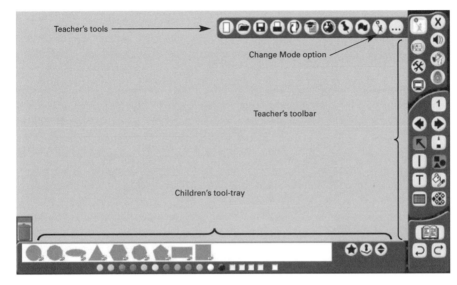

Figure 3.3. Overview of the ACTIVprimary™ flipchart

Returning to the flipchart view, it is important to realise from the outset that this view contains two modes, design mode and presentation mode. To shift between modes you click the 'Teachers' tools' menu button and select the 'Change Mode' option from the menu that appears as a result. To reverse this mode change you simply repeat the process. The Change Mode button will be yellow (as depicted in Figure 3.3) while the system is in presentation mode, but will show red in design mode. We will stay in presentation mode for the time being.

The tools

The top section of the side panel presents a series of general tools including the buttons that allow you to toggle between modes. In addition to this there are buttons for:

 Recording and playing sounds

 Accessing preset activities

 Clearing the screen completely or just of annotations or objects

Accessing useful tools

 Interacting with voting systems

 Toggling between Windows and flipchart view

Of these perhaps the only button that requires further discussion is the Useful Tools option. This menu contains a number of tools that might find a role in your classroom activities. For example, the Ruler tool places a semi-transparent but clearly calibrated rule on the flipchart, which can then be selected and manipulated like any other object on the screen. The Dice-rolling tool provides a simulation of dice rolling and the clock face provides an attractive facility for time-keeping. The best way to familiarise yourself with these tools is to just explore this menu and start thinking about when such facilities might be used effectively.

Of greater importance, perhaps, is the Snapshot tool, which is invoked by clicking on a button that bears a camera icon. The Camera tool itself allows the user to capture a snapshot of any region of the screen that they choose. The default setting is to record the contents of a rectangular area defined by a click-and-drag operation. However, a small up–down arrow button next to the Capture button allows you to toggle between other settings as well. You may define the area by clicking a number of boundary points or with a freehand line.

 The Snapshot button – invokes:  the Capture tool

Adding content

In the next panel down, we find what might be characterised as the drawing and annotation tools. Here the thinking behind the interface design becomes clear, for each time one of these tools is selected, a distinctive 'tool-tray' appears along the bottom of the screen, putting a relevant selection of controls within reach of a child user. In the depiction of the interface in Figure 3.3, you can see that the 'Draw shapes' tool is selected from the lower of the two side panels. This is signified by its being highlighted in red. As a result of this the bottom panel or 'tool-tray' is currently displaying the shapes that a user can create and a list of colours that can be applied to them.

You can also see that three other buttons are located apart from the rest on the right-hand side of the tool-tray. These resemble a star, a rubber stamp and a pair of arrowheads. These are known as 'additional options' and each tool-tray has a something similar. Here, the star allows you to control the thickness of the outlines of your shapes, the rubber stamp allows you to go into a mode where each pen-click creates a clone of the last shape you created, and the up and down arrow lets you choose from a bigger range of shapes. It is a good idea to explore the tool-trays and the additional options as this will make you more efficient and more flexible in what you do. In every case clicking the button for an additional option a second time effectively turns that tool off, restoring the system to its normal settings.

In addition to drawing shapes and lines the side toolbar also provides tools for:

 Moving between pages (and accessing new ones)

 Drawing freehand

 Typing text

 Filling continuous areas of space with colour

 Inserting backgrounds of various colours and patterns

 Inserting a grid as a background

In this way you can start to introduce content into your presentation very quickly. Of course richer content, imported from photo editors, say, from other Windows applications or from the internet can be cut and pasted into the presentation too (see below). You can also use the stylus, when you are in annotation mode, to create freehand annotations or drawings. Anything introduced in this way will be treated as a separate object and can be manipulated in a variety of ways.

Manipulating content

If you click on one of the options on a tool-tray for that tool, an object of that type – a line, a shape or a background, say – appears on the content area. In these cases the system immediately reverts to mouse mode, which is to say it assumes that you will then want to move the object you have created or manipulate it some other way. Similarly, any content that is pasted in from outside the ACTIVprimary™ application is treated in the same way. You will see that the object itself is selected and that a number of handles will be visible around it. These allow you to resize, rotate and sometimes distort the shape. Tapping on any object within the content area will cause it to become 'selected'.

The freehand drawing tool and the text tool are slightly different in the sense that the selections you make in the tool-tray do not cause any content to appear, but affect the thickness and colour of the line, if you go on to draw, or the character and style of the text if you then type. Similarly, the tool-tray for the dropper tool simply provides a means of choosing a colour that will be introduced once the user taps on a region of continuous space within the screen.

Another important consideration to bear in mind when using the freehand drawing tool is that once you have started, you need a way to tell the system to stop drawing, and an effective way of doing this is to click the Selector button, which is located on the same region of the side toolbar and is depicted at the top of page 28.

 Selector button

This is not the end of it, for you can manipulate your objects in other ways. However, we have gone as far as we can in presentation mode and we need to change to design mode before we can go further. To do this, simply click on the 'Teachers Tools' button (Figure 3.3) and select the 'Change Mode' button in order to enter design mode. You are now able to summon more editing options and do so by 'right-clicking' on an object in your presentation. This causes a menu like the one in Figure 3.4 to appear.

Figure 3.4. An object selected in the ACTIVprimary™ application

There are eight directional handles that let you resize and re-proportion your shape; a small box just to the right, which can be dragged clockwise or anticlockwise to achieve rotation; and the pop-up menu. This menu contains the option to lock, which means it cannot be accidentally moved or transformed in any way; or unlock, to reverse the lock instruction and change layer.

The layer that an object occupies dictates what covers what in cases of overlap, and you have the option to move the selected object to the front or to the back of the presentation, or to move it backwards and forwards one step at a time. Finally, you can 'Lock on Background', which will lock the object and move it onto the same layer as the background.

Unavailable in this example are the two options to 'Make Tickertape' and 'Deconstruct Word'. These are only available when the selected object is a piece of editable text. These allow you to make a piece of text move across the top or bottom of the screen like tickertape, or to break a sentence or phrase into separate words. You perform the latter task by right-clicking on a particular word within a text object and selecting the 'Deconstruct Word' option. A copy of that specific word will then appear.

Of course this leads us to consider text. You may very well have noticed that you have a button on your side panel that allows you to type in text. When writing like this you can set font, point size and colour by using the bottom tool-tray. However, you will want to write free-hand as well, especially in classroom situations, and you may well want to be able to convert these annotations into 'editable' or 'typed' text.

Writing is easy, as you simply tap the button for the Pencil tool and then write directly onto the board with your stylus. However, converting text to type is a slightly more complicated procedure. Here you must tap the button for the 'Recognise Text' tool, which is located in the 'Special Tools' tool-tray (see Figure 3.3). This then opens a dialogue box within which you write freehand. The system attempts to recognise what you are writing as you go along. Once you accept the translation it places the typed text onto your flipchart.

Conclusion

This has been a fairly condensed and breathless walk-through, and we will encounter some more tools, like spotlights and magnifiers, later on. However – as the following directed task is intended to demonstrate – once you have internalised what you have been shown so far, you should be ready to create and deliver exciting presentations. The bad news is that you now face the hardest task of all: designing useful and interactive classroom presentations. The good news is that the following chapters will provide you with considerable help in this.

PRACTICAL TASK PRACTICAL TASK **PRACTICAL TASK** PRACTICAL TASK **PRACTICAL TASK**

You may need to refer back at times and you will certainly need to think creatively around the broad instructions provided.

The objective here is to create a resource that allows all the children in a class to come up to the board and move a star of their preferred colour into a defined region. Having done this, you will move the chosen stars into a new slide and organise them into columns, finally replacing the columns with solid 'bars', modelling the representation of data onto a chart. You will need to make two slides to support this activity and they should resemble 1 and 2 in Figure 3.5.

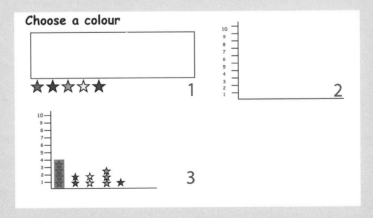

Figure 3.5. Creating a bar chart

You will need to consider how to duplicate the shapes of each colour so that a number of children can select the shape of the same colour, how to construct your y-axis so that the calibrations occur at regular intervals, and how to group and lock components of each template so that they can't be inadvertently disturbed. Do you need to consider the order of any of these components or does the way that the exercise runs ensure that this is unproblematic?

Finally, rehearse the exercise so that you end up with something resembling 3. Try to anticipate problems and ways in which the exercise could be improved.

A SUMMARY OF KEY POINTS

After reading this chapter you should be aware of the following:

> the importance of core generic operations such as taking and saving snapshots of your work;
> how to start building presentations;
> how to introduce content and how content is 'viewed' by IWB software applications;
> ways of manipulating objects;
> ways of composing, ordering and grouping objects;
> ways of creating hyperlinks to content located elsewhere.

4

The interactive whiteboard in school and in the classroom

By the end of this chapter you should:

- understand the organisational issues associated with using the IWB in the early years and primary classroom;
- apply a range of appropriate strategies using the IWB to early years and primary lessons;
- understand how a multimodal approach can be adapted to enhance the learning of the children you work with.

Professional Standards for QTS

This chapter addresses the following Professional Standards for QTS:

Q8, Q10, Q14, Q16, Q17, Q23, Q25, Q30

Introduction

This chapter examines the process of planning for the use of an IWB in early years and primary classrooms. It addresses the considerastions arising from the environment provided by the classroom itself and the likely impact that these will have on your teaching. There are two overriding principles pertaining to planning that run throughout this discussion:

- maximising the effectiveness of the whiteboard in your teaching;
- the implementation of strategies that ensure that this technology has the optimum effect on the learning of the children in your class.

Integrating the IWB into your lessons

The IWB is an engaging and potentially powerful tool. However, as with any tool, it is only of any benefit when it is used appropriately and in a way that adds value to your teaching. This is a consideration that should inform your use of the IWB, but even the most careful planning and the most imaginative development will count for nothing if certain organisational matters are not addressed. These relate to issues such as the positioning of the board, seating arrangements and the structuring and planning of sessions.

Factors affecting organisational strategies

There is no single guiding principle that determines how best to locate the IWB in relation to yourself or the children in your class. Rather there are a number of organisational strategies that could be adopted and you should always be prepared to adopt the one that best suits the learning task in hand. The way you organise the space available to you will determine how the children relate to the technology, and more importantly, to you as a teacher and to the content of the session. It will affect how much progress is made and how effectively you manage the transitions in your sessions.

An obvious, but often overlooked, prerequisite for successful use of the IWB is that it is accessible and that all the children have a clear line of sight to the board regardless of where they are seated. Obviously this may not always be easily achieved in reception or primary classrooms, where many children have their backs to the board because of the layout of the desks. It can also be difficult to seat large groups of children elsewhere as carpeted areas are often small. However, there are steps that can be taken to limit the impact of such pitfalls. For example, you should be able to anticipate which children are less able to deal with the disruption and inconvenience of having to turn to see the board and seat them accordingly. It is also true that children seated on the flanks of a class are likely to have a less clear view of a projected image. Again, it is difficult to entirely dispense with this problem, but you can minimise its impact by organising tables in such a way that the more marginal groups of children are located further back from the board. Also be aware of the children sitting in these places, and ensure that you take steps to fully engage them in the lesson. This can be through targeted question-and-answer techniques or by ensuring that you invite these children to come to the board when there is an opportunity to use it.

You can also address these issues in the way that you design and deliver IWB activities themselves. The clarity and size of the images and the point size of the text you use are important considerations, which often demand that you take conscious steps to ensure that everything is clearly visible, even from the back of the room. It is easy to forget this, particularly when working under a degree of stress, for example in a new classroom situation or while anticipating a lesson observation.

Managing the organisation of IWBS

Imagine you are working alone at a laptop computer to produce the slides that you will present to the class. You then may stand at the board to practise the lesson, but never adopt the perspective of a child who is seated in a remote location. An effective remedy is to run through your activity, pausing at intervals in order to sit in a range of places around the classroom. Not only will this give you an impression of the view that the children have of the board, but it will also allow you to establish that the children are able to read text and identify key features of any images that you display. Remember you can resize elements of your presentation during its delivery and with careful planning and rehearsal – anticipating key moments or elements within the activity where it may be necessary to draw attention to something – you can use this facility to great effect.

When designing the activity you should also consider the area of the board that the children can reach. The height at which an IWB is installed in a class inevitably reflects a compromise between the needs of the adult and those of the child users. In some classrooms you may find yourself stooped or sitting uncomfortably on the floor, while the children enjoy full access. In other situations you may find that you are able to operate comfortably and that the board is high enough to be visible throughout the classroom, but that children are only able to reach the lower regions of the board.

Because of these considerations it is not possible to devise a presentation that can be used effectively in all situations. You will find that adapting your slides to the size of the children and the height at which your board is installed becomes quite natural. However, you do have to have a good understanding of what they are capable of beforehand and how high they are comfortably able to reach.

Classroom organisation

You will be familiar with the approaches suggested here from other aspects of your teaching. However, the intention here is to enable you to incorporate the IWB and its use into your considerations. It is important that the children should be able to use the IWB and to this end you should ensure that there is sufficient space for the children to approach the board and to gather around it. If the children are sitting in their seats it is likely that they will all be able to see the board. If this is not the case, consider moving the children so that they are seated in an open 'U' shape, rather than a closed 'O'. They will still then have the benefits from being able to discuss the work as a table group without the problems associated with children having their backs to the board.

A key advantage of this arrangement is that it provides for easy movement around the class and ensures that all children are able to access the IWB with equal ease. However, it also means that some children will have a better view of the board than others. This approach will also lend itself more readily to a formal style of teaching as the opportunities to engage with the children on a more personal level are limited.

Another approach is to seat the children in a group around the whiteboard, as with an introduction to a story or lesson with younger children. It must be remembered that if a group of children is located near the board, a larger proportion of them will be viewing it from an acute angle. The relationships between elements in a presentation may also be less clear than if viewed from a greater distance and children may feel more inhibited for being crowded together. However, this arrangement makes it easy to guide the children and the teacher can engage with them more readily. Most importantly, the children are able to use the board more quickly in response to questions or points made by the teacher.

Equality of opportunity

In an inclusive classroom it is imperative that all children are given the same opportunity to access the IWB and benefit from its use. The field is wide. Areas which may be of particular concern will be those involving visual acuity, impaired mobility and the effects of dyslexia.

Over the course of your teacher education you are likely to encounter a number of children who will require that you adapt your use of the IWB to their needs. Examples could be creating access opportunities for wheelchair users and adapting text to suit dyslexic or visually impaired children. It is important to remember that children who have special educational needs will already have strategies put into place to support them by the school. Those children who have a statement of special educational needs will also have individual educational plans (IEPs). If it is appropriate these may well feature elements which relate to the use of the IWB. The advice offered here is to ensure that you are fully aware of any such issues within the classroom and to identify the impact that these have on the use of the IWB. A general recommendation is to observe how the class teacher uses the IWB with their class. An understanding of this existing use is essential when applied to children with special educational needs, as consistency can be important in itself.

Organisational checklist

- **Where can the children reach on the board?**
- **Are the children seated so that they can see the board with ease?**
- **Which areas of the classroom have the worst visibility?**
- **Which areas of the classroom have no effective visibility?**
- **Can the children move to and around the IWB?**
- **Are there any issues associated with equality of access and children's IEPs?**
- **Are the seating arrangements appropriate to continuity within the session?**
- **Are the colour scheme and typeface of the slides clearly visible?**
- **Finally, it might be worth creating a sketch map of the classroom in relation to the board to illustrate these organisational points.**

Using the whiteboard in the lesson

The whiteboard should be used in all aspects of the lesson. As a result of your own experience as learners, you will probably be familiar with the traditional approach according to which children or students focus on some form of display device at the front of the classroom. This may be a simple chalk board or images displayed by means of an overhead or multimedia projector (OHP, MMP). Towards the end of this chapter we will ask you to complete an activity where you identify ways in which the IWB can be used at each stage of a teaching session and it is worth bearing this in mind as you read the remainder of this section.

For present purposes we will adopt an approach which divides a session into the elements identified in the National Mathematics Strategy (2000). This is not to suggest that mathematics sessions offer the ideal structure of a lesson or a more appropriate context for the use of an IWB than any other subject area. Rather, they are used only for illustrative purposes.

The National Mathematics Strategy prescribes four distinct elements within a session. As you will probably be aware, these are the mental starter, the whole-class introduction, individual/group tasks and the plenary. Each of these elements of the session has different characteristics and offers different opportunities to the user of an IWB. We shortly move on to consider these, starting with a consideration of the theoretical context.

RESEARCH **SUMMARY**

Multimodal approaches to teaching using ICT

Multimodality is best viewed from the position of traditional media, where attention tends to be focused upon one form – print, photographs or sound (radio/music), for example – at a time. Traditional text will be read (in the case of English), top left to bottom right. Diagrams and activities may be inserted, but generally the reader receives the information in what we could term a passive manner, moving from one to another in a fixed order prescribed by the author. Compare this to the experience of someone exploring the internet. The reader encounters text that affords opportunities to leap to other parts of the website or the internet. He or she is likely to have the option to view explanatory animations or video clips via hyperlinks. That is to say, multimedia components can be introduced to a piece of text without interfering with its coherency and without intruding upon the reading experience itself. Readers enjoy a more active role and their experience is guided by choices they make.

This is an increasingly important part of our, and of our pupils' experience both inside and beyond the classroom. This is what is termed multimodality. Kress (2000) has attempted to put this into the context of the school classroom and the variety of means of communication that teachers have open to them when delivering sessions (Blight *et al*, 2005). Good examples of multimodal texts can be found on the BBC news website by searching for recent significant news events at **www.bbc.co.uk/news**

This resonates with the experience of most people working in schools. We are surrounded by multimodal texts. Since the introduction of the QCA Schemes of Work (1999) it has been acknowledged that children will engage in the creation of multimodal texts through the creation of hyperlinks and slide shows created in readily available software applications. A glance through Chapter 9 will give an indication of the variety of media that is now becoming accessible to children in school. We need hardly mention the media encountered in the home, including games, satellite TV and personal computers. The challenge is applying this multimodality in the classroom.

There is a recognition that adopting a variety of approaches promotes effective learning, reflecting the acknowledgement of the need to accommodate multiple intelligences (Gardner, 1999). Multimodal approaches to teaching offer a variety of modes to deliver and reinforce learning to minds that respond best to different stimuli. This is not the exclusive preserve of ICT, and more traditional methods and other forms of visual aids can be effective. However, IWBs offer a powerful tool for the development and delivery of a multimodal approach to teaching.

Teaching about ICT/teaching using ICT

We should pause a moment to consider the distinction between teaching about ICT and teaching using ICT. Teaching about ICT focuses on understanding the operation and functionality of the technology. In the case of the IWB this could involve knowing how to use the eraser function or the effect of specific actions involving the pens or styli. Learning using ICT, on the other hand, should not distract from the objective of the session, be this mathematics, history or design and technology. To use a specific example, children engaged in a group activity where they read together and then, with the support of a teacher, mark up the text for editing or redrafting are quite clearly using the technology to support subject-based learning. In some instances it is legitimate to teach an aspect of the function and operation in order to enable the children to focus on the subject-oriented activity. However, it should be remembered that the objective for this session will be an ICT objective, and if possible could feature as a theme or lesson within an ICT session. Trainees and NQTs can easily confuse the two, which demonstrates a lack of clarity in the purpose of their sessions and should be avoided.

We shall now turn to the task of exploring the role of an IWB in a four-part mathematics session.

Mental warm-up

During this phase of the session it is likely that you will use the IWB to present a series of questions or explore supporting information. Examples might be number squares, specifically created activities, calculators or some form of random-number generator. Pace is an important aspect at this stage and will depend upon the approach taken by the class teacher or trainee. As a result you would be less likely to require the children to be using the IWB themselves as this might slow proceedings. The emphasis will be upon completing the mathematical task in hand. To this end, you would be very likely to use a number of the features of the whiteboard software to ensure that maximum benefit was derived in the time available.

You might use the blinds or the eraser function to gradually reveal numbers in a number set, or present a number square that can be used as the basis for calculations, annotated in the process and very quickly reused in order to reinforce understanding of a process. You might use a random-number generator to provide the integers requiring multiplication or subtraction or you might obtain ready-made activities, such as animated number lines.

You will find that there is a wealth of electronic and non-electronic resources available to support this element of the session. Often non-electronic versions can be adapted for use with the IWB through scanning or translation, but you will find a great deal on the internet as well.

If we were to try to extrapolate a single objective here, one that could be applied across subject areas, we might say that we were seeking to use the IWB to enhance traditional approaches and activities. The teacher might remain at the front of the classroom and present resources to the class. These resources form the basis of a teaching or learning activity to which the children respond and the activities themselves would be familiar to previous generations. The IWB may make the teacher more efficient and, used properly, can make the activity more engaging. However, it is important to remember that in addition to the teacher's mastery of the technology, it is their capacity to identify and create supportive resources and their capacity to interact in an appropriate way with the children that ensures the effectiveness of this part of the session.

Whole-class session

As a presentational device the IWB setup can be overlooked because of its resemblance to a projector and a static screen. Too often, in whole-class sessions, it is not used in an interactive way. Earlier chapters have considered the wide and exciting opportunities that the IWB can offer the teacher and the children as a support for teaching and learning. This is the key part of the lesson and it is here that the whiteboard can really come into its own.

A good starting point is to consider how you would try to teach well if you were equipped with a static whiteboard or flipchart. If this was the case, what would you present to the children as visual aids? What would you do to illustrate your key point? How would you present text to the children? How would you reinforce the learning objectives? Once you have considered this you can begin to consider the ways in which the IWB can be used.

The software that comes with your IWB affords you the luxury of being able to pre-prepare slides in a structured way and this gives you the opportunity to present ideas in a crisp sequence. However, you could achieve this equally with a PowerPoint presentation and would not really need to use more than the most basic and least interactive features in order to deliver it. As with a PowerPoint presentation, the less positive aspect of this kind of resource is the rigid sequencing that it imposes upon the lesson and this would be particularly detrimental in a primary or early years classroom, where you would ideally aim to encourage and respond to the reactions of the children.

Rather than imposing a structure on the lesson you should aim to explore every relevant avenue that emerges from your class's engagement with the learning process, however unexpected. Here the IWB comes into its own for in addition to being able to incorporate rich graphical, animated and even multimedia content into your visual aids you are also able to manipulate and build upon them in the course of the lesson. The IWB allows your class to interact with the presentation and to develop it into a unique record of their learning journey in the process.

Individual/group activities

The individual/group activities element is often the time when a session fails to exploit the maximum the potential of the IWB. If we accept that the IWB is a powerful (and costly) learning tool, we should also accept that this power should not only reside in the hands of the class teacher. We would urge you to explore activities and ways of integrating the equipment and software into this aspect of your lessons, promoting the unsupervised use of the IWB by your class.

Children can quite happily and confidently engage in tasks on the whiteboard, either individually or in groups. They can do so under the supervision of an adult, but this supervision often needs only to be imposed in order ensure that children follow the task in hand. We would recommend that if children are using the board, they should be given a very clear set of guidelines indicating what they should do and clear instructions detailing how the task is to be conducted. Examples of these 'rules' could be:

* **one person only to hold the stylus/pen;**
* **don't press on the board too hard;**
* **use only this toolbar or that palette to achieve this or that objective;**
* **what action to take should they inadvertently move away from the selected program or software, or make some other kind of mistake.**

You will need to speak to the class teacher and/or the ICT co-ordinator to discuss any guidelines that your placement school has in place for when children use the IWB. Before you plan a session in which you expect the children to use the IWB it would be wise to consider how you would implement these guidelines or guidelines of your own, in order to encourage appropriate use and to constrain inappropriate use of the board.

As the IWB is essentially a means of sharing information and ideas, you should think carefully about whether setting individual tasks is the best use of this facility. Children working in groups around the IWB will behave in much the same way as they do in other areas of their school life. Initially, due to the novelty of using the board, behaviour may well exhibit a high level of enthusiasm and commensurately low level of self-control. For this reason it is often useful to set some form of task where the children are encouraged to become acquainted with the touch and operation of the board. Your own experiences of learning to use the IWB will be relevant here. This is where we need to consider the way in which learning about ICT supports us in engaging children's learning with ICT.

In order to familiarise the children with the use of the board as part of a set of lessons, it may be worthwhile introducing some sort of activity that is related to the subject area/theme and the anticipated future tasks; for example, a simple interactive teaching program (ITP) or adapting already created slides. However, once you have established rules and guidelines and once you have equipped the children with the basic skills and the confidence they need, you should find they require little more than a minimum of supervision, where you decide that this is appropriate.

As with any guided activity, the nature of the task and child interaction will be different if adults are used to support it. These activities should encourage the children to engage in open-ended tasks that encourage discussion and problem-solving. Where any kind of super-vision is required it is important that, if you are not the adult supporting the group using the board, you are confident that the adult who is responsible is competent at using the software and features of the board that are involved in the task. For this reason it is best to ensure that time is available to brief the leading adult.

In summary, the independent or group use of the IWB can often be neglected. It should be encouraged wherever possible as this can capitalise on the benefits of the technology for targeted children. However, it is important to remember that you ensure that both the children and any adult staff supporting them have the technological competence to support the learning activity.

Plenary

Again, the efficiency that the IWB offers makes it particularly useful in developing a coherent and effective plenary. The purpose of the plenary is to revise the key points of the session and then look forward to the development of the skills or knowledge. This reinforcement is seen as a critical part of the lesson structure. One of the signal benefits of using an IWB, a benefit that is particularly great if resources have been planned and developed in a creative way that anticipates and supports interaction by the learners, is that presentations grow into an engaging record of teaching and learning as the lesson progresses. They can then by used to indicate and emphasise key lesson points and, perhaps more importantly, key features of the stages and processes through which these points were attained.

This can result in a saving of time that can be used to create reinforcement tasks to be deployed in the introduction of future sessions. However, the 'record of learning' as it was described in the previous paragraph can often stand as an attractive and engaging resource in its own right; one that can be simply and easily printed, copied and distributed to the class. An incidental advantage of doing this is that you can then restore the electronic version of the presentation to its original state, whereupon it is ready to be used again on the next occasion you deliver the lesson.

PRACTICAL TASK PRACTICAL TASK PRACTICAL TASK PRACTICAL TASK PRACTICAL TASK

Using the structure of the session described above, consider ways in which the IWB can be used to support teaching and learning for a theme in a specific subject area. It can be the case that trainees who are not familiar with the technology may not have the opportunity to consider ways in which it can support their work. This activity will help you focus on the possible support that can be provided. As we noted earlier, it is critical that, when teaching using ICT, your starting point for the activity is the learning objective. By considering in detail how you could use the IWB you can then incorporate the ideas into your planning, using the school approved format. You may wish to re-read other sections of the book to help you in the completing of the activity.

SUBJECT: _____

THEME: _____

OBJECTIVE: _____

_____

Stage of lesson	Activity	Teacher involvement	Pupil involvement	Notes
Warm-up/Starter				
Introduction				
Independent/ Group work				
Plenary				

Earlier we considered the link between learning theory and the use of IWBs. This emphasised the impact on children's learning. In this chapter we are beginning to consider the impact that this will have on your teaching.

CLASSROOM STORY **CLASSROOM** STORY CLASSROOM STORY **CLASSROOM STORY**

Hannah is an experienced teacher who is teaching design and technology to a group of Year 4 children in a large suburban primary school. The school is well resourced; this extends to the ICT available for the children. The sequence of sessions is related to the production of pop-up books. The objective of this lesson is that the children will be able to make a pop-up hinge. The lesson begins with Hannah using the whiteboard to display the session objectives and summary. She uses the pen to highlight key words and question the children to establish understanding. She then revises the different forms of folds that the children have encountered in this series of lessons. This uses the slide that formed the revision part of the plenary for the last session. As a final reinforcement she presents the children with a list of names of several folds and hinges and some images of the same. She then invites two children to come out to the IWB to join the name with the appropriate diagram. Satisfied that she has effectively revised the previous sessions, she moves on to her main introduction. Initially she demonstrates the type of hinge that is the focus of today's session. She does this by reading the story in a pop-up book which ends with this hinge.

▶

There is a pause in the lesson as the children ask for the story to be re-read. Once this is complete, Hannah returns to the whiteboard, which has been displaying the front cover of the book while she reads the story. She then gives a set of instructions describing how the hinge can be made. This is presented in sequence, accompanied by pictures of each stage. She then turns to her classroom assistant, who models the activity as the slides are re-run. The slide sequence then returns to the beginning. Once again the sequence is modelled as the slides are run. However, this time Hannah draws on the board to emphasise key points relating to the folding and cutting of the paper.

The children are now tasked with creating their own hinge. They are supported in this by the teaching assistant, who works with groups of children at the whiteboard, discussing each stage with them and comparing their efforts with the model provided by the slides. The lesson concludes and the children gather around the whiteboard for the plenary. The objectives are revised; the existing cuts and folds are presented on the IWB. They are quickly discussed and Hannah then revises the key points of the day's session. She then clicks on a link which operates the webcam. This is positioned so that examples of children's work can be viewed on the IWB. Hannah invites the children to comment on the examples they have seen, and as the children make their comments Hannah writes down some key points on the screen. These are then printed out for future use. To conclude, Hannah shows the children a photograph of the next activity, combining the various folds into their own pop-up book.

This story illustrates the way in which an IWB can be incorporated into an essentially practical session. There is evidence of a multimodal approach being adopted, and good use is made of the unique features of the whiteboard. Other adults are incorporated into the session and children are encouraged to evaluate their own work.

A SUMMARY OF KEY POINTS

After reading this chapter you should now be aware of these key points:

> classroom layout and the arrangement of seating are influenced by the use of the IWB and the nature of the task;
> the IWB can be used in different ways depending on the stage of the lesson;
> the aim should be to maximise the use of the whiteboard – this can be done through guided group activities or individual use;
> the most effective teaching using this technology adopts a multimodal approach.

5

Theoretical underpinnings and pedagogical themes

By the end of this chapter you should:

- understand how IWBs can enhance your own teaching;
- understand how IWBs can help children learn effectively;
- understand different levels of interaction;
- start to address how IWBs can be used for different groups of learners.

Professional Standards for QTS

This chapter addresses the following Professional Standards for QTS:

Q7, Q14, Q17, Q23, Q25

Introduction

Previous chapters have mainly concentrated on the technical and operational issues relating to the use of an IWB. It is important that you are confident using the technology, as this will help you become a more assured and effective user of it. However, this chapter seeks to extend your understanding of IWBs by examining pedagogical themes and exploring how teaching and learning might be enhanced with the use of this technology.

IWBs are much more than just 'flashy' pieces of equipment that perform a range of tricks. They can never take the place of a good teacher, but when used effectively they can support even the best teaching in a number of ways. This chapter seeks to explore and assess the power of the IWB so that you can harness its potential and maximise the use of this technology.

Engagement and motivation

IWBs appear to have considerable appeal to people of all ages, which can reveal itself in increased engagement and an improvement in the motivation of those who use them. Used properly, an IWB can offer teachers new opportunities for the presentation of materials in the classroom. It allows a presentation to become more dynamic and to incorporate a greater range of media, engaging more senses in something that resembles an almost cinematic experience. Upon seeing the technology for the first time my own response, as a teacher and ICT co-ordinator, was that I simply had to have one in the classroom. Here was a piece of equipment that could present materials in a sophisticated manner that competed with the technology children encountered in their lives outside school.

The creative opportunities IWBs offered to me as a teacher were not to be missed – it made my teaching more enjoyable and varied and the reaction of the class to the use of the board was very satisfying. Factors that appear key to increased engagement and motivation include:

- **the ability to combine different materials in order to make teaching more dynamic and stimulating;**
- **the ability to move and manipulate objects;**
- **the involvement of the children in coming to the board and 'making things happen'.**

RESEARCH **SUMMARY**

Levy (2002) conducted a small-scale research project that examined the attitudes of teachers and children to IWB technology in two Sheffield secondary schools. The teachers in the school commented that IWBs made learning 'more entertaining' and that the children were 'much engaged'. Children also expressed their approval by using terms like 'fun' and 'exciting', saying that they were more interesting than normal whiteboards. Smith (2001) also pointed to increases in enthusiasm and motivation generated by the use of IWBs, not just among children, but also among staff. What is more, research by the North Islington Education Action Zone (2002) suggests that IWBs improved behaviour and encouraged children to pay attention for longer. They even made claims that IWBs contributed to higher levels of attainment as a result. Cuthell (2005) has linked IWBs with 'ludic' or 'play' elements. He points out that play is an important element of learning and that IWBs can effectively combine serious intentions with fun, thereby further engaging the children who use them.

Learning styles

Over the last 10 years there has been much emphasis on how learning styles relate to a child's ability to understand and assimilate new concepts. There has been an acknowledgement that the use of different types of delivery in a lesson can increase its overall appeal, as it caters for different types of learner as a result. As a consequence many teachers have sought to adapt and broaden their teaching strategy in order to assimilate this.

It is thought that children will respond to this taught material in a variety of ways depending on their learning preference. An emphasis on recognising different learning styles is current in schools today and many initial teacher training (ITT) courses now include materials of this type. There are numerous models that seek to define a child's learning style, including the Learning Styles Inventory by Dunn *et al* (1975–1997) and Howard Gardner's Multiple Intelligences (1999). The VAK model suggests that sensory receivers can dominate learning and though learners will all use visual, auditory and kinaesthetic senses, any given individual might rely on one more than the others. For instance, if a child has a kinaesthetic preference they might learn best by doing, manipulating and moving objects, as opposed to a visual learner who likes to receive information by reading text and looking at diagrams. The term 'tactile' is often associated with 'kinaesthetic' learning and refers particularly to touching devices. For some, however, this represents a fourth category in its own right and they would argue for an extension of the acronym to VAKT.

Learning styles and their validity are subject to some controversy in academic fields and recently the use the VAK/T model, which is so popular in schools, has been called into question (Sternberg *et al*, 2001; Coffield *et al*, 2004; Sharp *et al*, 2006). This school of thought asserts that the model is oversimplistic and liable to encourage a situation in which teachers label children as being restricted to one or another learning style.

There is not the space in this book to discuss the validity of learning styles, just to make you aware of the debate surrounding them. It can, however, be asserted with reasonable confidence that the best teaching engages a range of different senses and that this approach is particularly valuable with young learners. It is here that the IWB comes into its own, for this technology provides the ability to seamlessly combine large-scale graphics, animation, video and audio facilities. This results in their being able to reinforce the learning process in a way that is unavailable when using traditional whiteboards.

What is more, the fact that children can touch the board and manipulate information broadens the range of faculties that it engages. In particular, the IWB can aid 'kinaesthetic' learning, allowing the child to link verbal and visual information with active involvement through the manipulation and movement of objects under discussion. This is likely to have a positive impact on retention and engagement in class (Miller *et al*, 2005).

Pace of lessons

IWBs are reported to have a positive impact on the pace of a lesson. A teacher is able to make quicker progress through planned learning materials than when using more traditional teaching tools. The reason for this is the IWB's ability to manipulate models and illustrations in a way that was not previously possible. This reduces interruptions to the flow of one teaching point to the next when delivering prepared materials. This frees the teacher from becoming preoccupied with the management of resources, allowing them to focus on the teaching at hand. Levy (2002) found that teachers worked more efficiently, just by being able to summon resources from the IWB's libraries or from materials prepared prior to the lesson. This was shown to prevent time being wasted by tasks such as writing information on the board during the course of the lesson. This may seem mundane, but such details can result in great benefits in terms of efficiency.

Consider the logistics of teaching a history lesson with the aid of a series of pictorial resources from a textbook. The teacher would have to give out the books and possibly negotiate the sharing of texts if there were not enough to go around. The children would then have turn their attention between sheets and the teacher would have to ensure that the whole class was on the same page at regular intervals. This process would take up valuable time and would invite disruption. With the advent of the IWB these pictures can be scanned, rather than photocopied, and arranged on a slide or a series of slides, ready to be enlarged by the teacher as and when required. This would allow images to be compared alongside each other and even for details of one image to be examined in isolation, using the spotlight tools. In this way the

IWB extends what would be possible with a computer and data projector. Someone preparing such a lesson in PowerPoint would need to plan it in detail and would then find it difficult to deviate from that plan. With an IWB the images can be manipulated freely and can even be supplemented by annotations or other media imported from elsewhere.

Enhancing learning using IWBs

Thinking skills and ICT

There is a great deal of anecdotal evidence that suggests that IWBs somehow extends thinking and therefore learning; a consensus that might be taken to justify the tremendous investment in IWBs that has taken place over the last few years. Are we to believe that the technology itself confers some benefit upon teachers and learners by virtue only of its presence in the classroom? Of course the answer is no, for the technology is only an agent in the learning process, a medium that becomes effective only when employed appropriately.

Consider the following example of teaching using ICT and the way it promotes thinking skills. Lessons using Logotron's LOGO, where children have to program a turtle to move around a screen, provide an example where children learn to make a piece of technology function. However, in doing so children are learning far more than how to operate the device itself. The real objective is to develop problem-solving skills; the ability to analyse a situation and apply specific skills or synthesise arguments in order to achieve a set objective.

The ICT involved in this learning situation requires more than just the application of learned skills and routines like cutting and pasting or entering data. The capability that the exercise attempts to develop is the ability to apply knowledge and experience of ICT to various learning scenarios (Potter and Darbyshire, 2005). Children need to participate in 'active learning' or 'learning by doing' and LOGO requires them to think and solve problems. Just getting a group of children to move a turtle in a square requires them to collaborate, experiment, revise original ideas, make mistakes, experience frustration and finally feel immense achievement when the group actually resolves the problem.

The approach outlined above depends on a teacher understanding how to make the most of teaching and learning using ICT and this can be applied to the way IWBs are used with a class. An IWB can be used to encourage children to ask 'what if' questions, for the moment they encounter one they want to touch and ask 'what happens if I try this?', 'why did that happen?', 'let me have a go' or 'let me be involved'. This instantaneous spirit of enquiry can be further enhanced by the introduction of animated, audio, video and online content. This can enable children to visualise sequences and learn in a way that was not previously available.

Put another way, if used in the correct manner an IWB helps children to construct meaning for themselves. Cuthell (2005) discusses a view of learning that compares it to a 'mosaic', where small pieces of information are gradually placed together to form meaning. An IWB's multi-sensory approach helps children to perceive a bigger picture through their introduction to and manipulation of smaller related fragments. This recalls the exploratory or constructivist paradigm, which places an emphasis on learning by a process of discovery rather than by the mechanical transference of information from teacher to pupil.

Levels of interaction

The ability to master an IWB depends on more than just mastery of the technology. It is also vital to manage the interaction between the children and the board effectively. A teacher must have a good understanding of how a board can be used and a working knowledge of interactive teaching in order to extract all potential learning opportunities.

Too often, use of the IWB fails to demonstrate its potential. For example, Microsoft PowerPoint can incorporate multimedia and can be seen clearly with cinematic effect without using an IWB. A few years ago this type of presentation of information would have been impressive to the average primary school child. However, the 'wow' factor involved here soon pales and it could be argued that presentations of this sort become tedious if used repeatedly. Many of us have sat through overlong PowerPoint presentations that use too many bulleted points or present too much raw information that is rendered no more digestible for it being interspersed with the odd graphic. Here, the levels of interaction are very basic and so the learner remains passive.

This form of use has been coined as 'supported didactic' teaching (Miller *et al*, 2005) and it would be questionable whether the investment in the IWB was justified. However, it is also important to avoid the situation where the IWB is used only in order to exhibit the 'tricks' it offers for their own sake. A teacher can get over-involved in learning how to use visual tools when presenting the lesson. These 'effects' are indeed impressive, but can take time to prepare and risk blurring the line between drawing attention to a learning task and distracting children from it. More importantly, if use of the IWB only consists of the teacher invoking special effects, the children remain passive and will only stay engaged for so long.

Greater levels of interaction and subsequently more effective use of the IWB occur when the children are required to come to the board. Even then, just coming to the board once throughout the course of an entire session is not very likely to enhance the learning experience of that child. However, if the IWB is used to present some sort of problem which the child is then required to come to the board and solve via the manipulation of objects, a more effective learning situation might arise.

Materials that make use of 'drag and drop' facilities and require children to manipulate components in order to achieve a specific learning objective, support a more sophisticated kind of interaction. Alternatively, PowerPoint presentations can be enhanced by the use of 'action buttons' or other kinds of hyperlinks in order to include an element of choice or require decision-making and encourage a higher level of interaction (see Chapter 6 for a more in-depth explanation). The full potential of the board is used when it encourages the user to think in the context of an activity that they are conducting. Miller *et al* (2005) state that IWB activities that allow for a higher level of interaction include the following:

- **Drag and drop, e.g. sorting data into Venn diagrams or moving objects to fill in a pictogram.**
- **Hiding objects, e.g. using a solid shape to hide half of an image of a butterfly. The children would then draw the other half before the rest of the object is revealed, to see if the drawings match.**
- **The use of colouring and shading to give greater reinforcement of concepts.**
- **Matching activities, e.g. resources that require the children to match items like pairs of homophones or to create compound words. This could be achieved by moving them together or drawing lines with the pens provided.**
- **Controlling processes, e.g. providing animations that model a concept and provide the ability to change variables or parameters in order to test different situations. For example, an animation could be downloaded from the internet to show how blood is pumped around the heart.**

Dialogue and collaboration

One of the most powerful effects of the IWB is that it promotes a dialogue and collaboration between children and between them and the teacher. Enhanced speaking and listening opportunities lie at the heart of good IWB use. There appear to be three main reasons for this improved dialogic dimension.

- **The position of the board is critical. Before the advent of data projectors and IWBs, teaching whole classes with ICT could be a tiresome experience. Grouping large numbers of children around a small screen is logistically problematic and this often leads to children sitting around a screen, either individually or in small groups, without the teacher as a mediator. The arrival of IWBs resulted in the whole class being able to group themselves comfortably in front of the screen in the teacher's presence. This arrangement encourages a much more collaborative experience for the class.**
- **The presentation of multimedia materials that are used wisely and planned to allow for a problem-solving dimension stimulates thinking and demands interaction in order to achieve an agreed solution.**
- **The teacher who relinquishes control of the board to the children increases their involvement. When this transfer of power is combined with sophisticated questioning, the potential for interaction also increases. The teacher who moves to the back of the classroom and allows the children to model or peer-teach concepts, promotes a highly effective learning environment.**

RESEARCH **SUMMARY**

Graham (2003) used IWBs to promote learning through pre-prepared or web-based games. She found that the use of this technology resulted not only in enhanced understanding but increased participation from children she described as 'disaffected' or 'switched off'. Levy (2002) found the IWB's strong visual and conceptual appeal stimulated higher levels of participation and dialogue. The children who were the subjects of this study stated that they could use the boards to write on 'and talk at the same time'. Warren (no date given) argues for increased participation of children due to the ability to design materials for the IWB that are not 'complete' or providing all the answers. Children are then required to participate and discuss how to fill in the 'white spaces' and complete the information. The National Whiteboard Network (2004) concluded that whiteboards allow the teacher to spend more time on whole-class teaching, and noticed that the children talked for longer, using a wider range of vocabulary. They also highlight the board's ability to quickly change or reconfigure information, providing opportunities for engagement at a higher level with particular reference to analysis and interrogation.

REFLECTIVE TASK
ВЕFLECTIVE TASK

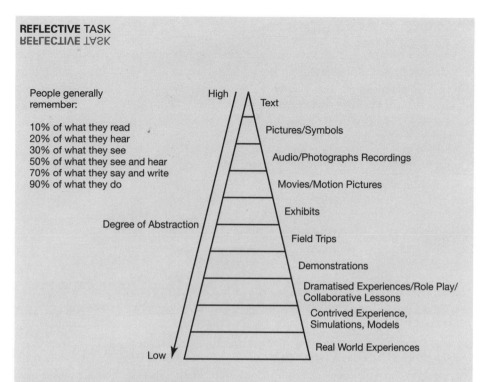

Figure 5.1. Dale's cone of experience

- **Consider Dale's 'cone of experience' (Figure 5.1). The teaching techniques towards the base of the cone are more likely to be the most effective learning situations.**
- **Evaluate your current teaching routines against the criteria on the cone.**
- **How does the use of an IWB help you achieve the criteria on the cone?**

Dale's cone of experience was produced by Edgar Dale in 1946. More information and another example of the cone can be found at **http://my-ecoach.com/idtimeline/1940s.htm** (accessed 13.10.06).

Interactive whiteboards and children with special educational needs

IWBs appear to be particularly effective at enhancing the learning experience of many children with special educational needs. Carter (2002) reports impressive benefits when using the IWB with deaf children. She noted the ease of delivering curriculum content where deaf children could view the material on the whiteboard with the teacher signing language at the same time. When previously completing the same task using a PC, children would have to look at the screen and then look at the teacher to sign for more information, making a segmented learning experience.

Visually impaired children can benefit from the larger images, text and icons provided by an IWB. Lee and Boyle (2003) advocate the benefits of using a scanner to transform A4 pages into very large images that can then be manipulated. They also used the recording facility of an IWB (SMART Board™) with SEN children. For instance, the IWB was used to assist hand-writing development by making a recording of the ways in which letters were formed, and replaying them in slow motion. A child could then watch this 'movie' as many times as they wished before practising the formation on the board themselves.

Clark and Cooper (2003) describe how an IWB was used to develop the language skills of deaf students. The whiteboard was used to model the English language visually, by colour coding words in sentences. This helped deaf students to understand sentence structure and individual word function. The students were subsequently able to demonstrate their understanding of grammar, by rearranging the sentences and changing the colour of words as their function in a sentence changed.

Interactive whiteboards and early years children

As long as the board is set at the correct height, this technology is particularly appealing to very young children. Cuthell (2005) attributes this to 'ostensiveness'. This term relates to the way young children learn by pointing to objects to reinforce concepts. The IWB allows members of a class not only to point at objects on the screen but to interact with them in doing so. For example, an object that is identified in this way, i.e. by being touched physically, can be set up to respond to the event, providing affirmation that it had been identified correctly. This interaction enhances the learning experience.

Cuthell also highlights the fact that the IWB models real-life experiences, where the child can manipulate objects in a way that was not previously possible. This provides an important bridge between concrete and more abstract learning methods.

Another advantage of using an IWB with early years children is that it removes the necessity to use complex input devices such as a mouse or keyboard in computer use. For children who are just learning to write, the requirement to find letters on a keyboard can be time consuming and imposes a potentially confusing step between building the word on a keyboard and seeing it formed on a screen. The IWB offers a solution to these conundrums by allowing children to write on a computer screen, just as they would write on paper. This allows them to concentrate on the word itself without being distracted by the mechanical task of locating the letters (Goodison, 2002, p288). Furthermore, children also find it tricky to co-ordinate drag-and-drop manoeuvres when using a mouse; a 'point and drag' technique is much more achievable for young children. The children can simply move objects with their finger or a stylus, taking away the requirement to keep a mouse button depressed while moving it at the same time.

CLASSROOM STORY **CLASSROOM** STORY CLASSROOM STORY **CLASSROOM STORY**

Jane wishes to deliver a science lesson via the IWB to a group of Foundation Stage children. Jane is a confident user of the IWB and would like to use some of its interactive elements to enhance the learning taking place.

Jane starts the lesson by getting the children to investigate a selection of different vegetables. She encourages the group to explore the foods and to describe them using terms like shiny, furry, prickly, smooth and rough.

The children were then shown a pre-prepared screen on the IWB where digital pictures of vegetables had been enlarged. The children were encouraged to predict what the food might look like if it were cut in half. Jane spent time encouraging the children to raise questions about the inside of the vegetables. The children made statements about what colour the insides might be, whether they would be hard or soft and if any of the foods contained seeds. They were asked to make annotations on top of the photographs to draw what might be inside each vegetable. The children then physically cut open the vegetables and examined their contents. The group moved on to make a detailed exploration of parts of the vegetables under the digital microscope. The whole group was able to be involved in this activity as the microscope was attached to the IWB and its display could therefore be seen by all, not just an individual. The group returned to the previous screen on the IWB and looked at their original predictive annotations. They discussed whether they had been right or wrong and Jane completed the activity by showing the children images of the vegetables cut in half.

PRACTICAL TASK PRACTICAL TASK PRACTICAL TASK PRACTICAL TASK PRACTICAL TASK

- **Go to the following website:** www.topmarks.co.uk/interactive.aspx#fmaths. **This website provides free resources for IWBs.**
- **Select the activities 'counting to twenty' 'big and small' and 'building blocks' and complete the tasks.**
- **Think about what is effective about these sites.**
- **Evaluate the level of interaction achievable by these sites.**
- **Evaluate whether the sites allow the user to manipulate objects.**
- **What could be improved on the sites – what might Foundation Stage children find difficult to achieve on these activities?**

Practical benefits to teachers

The vast majority of this chapter has been dedicated to discussing the pedagogical issues associated with IWBs. There are, however, some more practical advantages to teaching using this technology. An IWB can enable a teacher to plan and teach more efficiently. Resources can be saved to hard disk to be revised and edited for additional use on a future occasion. The ability to save whiteboard screens can also have a more immediate benefit during the course of a lesson, as a teacher can return to earlier pages to help a child who is late entering the lesson or to remind them of initial concepts. Saved work can be returned to in order to make links between ideas or to act as a revision aid at the start of the next lesson. Of particular note is the ability to save teacher annotations – ideas and notes that have been added during the course of a lesson and which can act as an invaluable prompt or source of ideas at a future date.

Prior to the use of IWBs it was common for teachers to have to save work for use in the next lesson on large, unwieldy flipchart paper or to ensure that it was not inadvertently wiped off the board. The IWB now makes it easy to save the collective thoughts of the class after a whole-class teaching session. Teachers have also reported more effective planning when using IWBs. Latham (2002) found that although planning initially took longer, the nature of IWBs made teachers take careful account of visual aspects of learning, most notably modelling and illustration, which in turn had a positive impact on their teaching.

A SUMMARY OF KEY POINTS

As a result of reading this chapter you should now be aware of the following:

> motivational factors and IWBs;
> learning styles and IWBs;
> improved teaching pace and IWBs;
> different levels of interaction when using an IWB;
> enhanced dialogue and collaboration when using an IWB;
> SEN and IWBs;
> early years and IWBs;
> practical benefits when planning and teaching.

6

Finding, evaluating and using resources

By the end of this chapter you should:

- match appropriate resources to a range of curriculum areas;
- evaluate resources;
- adapt resources;
- incorporate these resources into your lesson planning.

Professional Standards for QTS

This chapter addresses the following Professional Standards for QTS:

Q3, Q7, Q8, Q17, Q25, Q30

Introduction

In Chapter 8 discussion focuses on the freely available and commercially produced resources found on the internet, but these are not the only sources. There are software tools that must be paid for and provide an environment that is conducive for a wide range of teaching activities, and there are those resources which you or your colleagues create for yourselves. This chapter will focus on strategies that you can use to obtain and make the best use of such materials, whatever their origin. By its conclusion you should be able to make considered judgements about the selection and adaptation of resources to support your teaching in a constructive and appropriate way.

Before we begin, consider the range of resources that you have access to in the classroom. Take a moment to picture examples of the tools and resources that you might be called upon to use and you will probably think of things like chalk boards, overhead projectors, flipcharts and standard whiteboards, images, printed texts and physical artefacts or tools that can be used to model concepts. In addition there are all your internal resources, for yours is the crucial role and it falls upon you to draw the resources together into a coherent whole. You, the teacher, provide the links and the contextual information that render the resources you have assembled meaningful.

To be effective you should think in terms of exploiting all of these resources, whenever, but only when, they can be used constructively to achieve the ends set out in the curriculum. Proper evaluation should not only address the integral features of a resource or a tool, therefore, but should consider them in the environment created by other items of classroom apparatus, your own teaching style and the curriculum. ICT does not replace any of these things and it can only be effective when it complements them.

Evaluating resources

A good starting point for a discussion of this evaluation process is the government's advice and the support that they provide for investment in electronic resources. The government in England and Wales offers what they term 'e-credits'. This is a system which provides dedicated funds to schools for the purchase of software from government-approved suppliers and a certain number of credits are awarded to each school. These can be 'spent' as schools choose, providing they do so from an approved supplier, topping up the difference between the credits available to them and the cost of the software they have purchased from their own budget when necessary. This is an attempt by the government to ensure that schools are enabled and encouraged to purchase software while still retaining a relatively open market.

The following Department for Education and Skills (DfES) link will provide you with a good impression of the kinds of questions that should be asked when evaluating software to meet the needs of the whole school: **www.curriculumonline.gov.uk/Howto/EvaluatingResources.htm**

It is likely that the staff in your school will have gone through this and it is unlikely that you, as a trainee, will be in a position or have the time to influence the purchasing of software in the school. For this reason you will inevitably be limited in terms of the materials available to you. However, whatever resources you have, you will need to be able to evaluate their usefulness.

A framework for evaluation

This section and the follow-up activity will enable you to focus on your own evaluations when deciding on what resources to use when teaching. It will give you some points to consider when evaluating software and you should take into account the DfES approach that is described in the web page noted above. However, references have been adapted to the needs of the trainee classroom teacher.

Regardless of the approach that you use, you will need to ensure that all your decisions satisfy some core questions. These form the subheadings for the discussion that follows.

What curriculum do I have to deliver?

The starting point for any evaluation of educational software is a clear understanding of the curriculum and its objectives. It is this understanding that will drive your teaching and you should allow that to guide your choice of the software that you use with the children in your placement class. On a number of occasions the authors have encountered trainees attempting to use inappropriate software because impressive graphical or multimedia content has distracted them from a cool-headed evaluation of its appropriateness. This error may derive from the fact that clever software design has engaged the trainee's natural enthusiasm, in which case it is almost always the case that the initial impression pales as the lesson-planning process begins in earnest. More problematical, however, are cases when the error derives from a flawed understanding of the curriculum.

PRACTICAL TASK PRACTICAL TASK **PRACTICAL TASK** PRACTICAL TASK **PRACTICAL TASK**

To reinforce the link to the curriculum it is useful to examine other people's evaluations. These are often documented on the internet and you should pay particular attention to those that draw explicit links between features of the software and core learning and teaching objectives. Schoolzone, www.schoolzone.co.uk, offers a collection of free resources and claims, at the time of writing, to provide over 50,000 evaluations of learning materials.

What resources does the school already have?

Once you are clear about the requirements of the curriculum you can begin to consider a point that may seem trivial, but is important and too often overlooked. Towards the end of this chapter we consider a piece of software called Kar2ouche. This is an engaging and useful teaching resource. You are likely to have encountered it as part of your course, and may have been delighted with the results. If so you are likely to be keen to use it as part of your next placement and the authors have frequently been required to advise trainees who have begun to plan ICT activities for their teaching prior to gaining a full impression of their placement school and its resources. The problem is that the school may not possess the software that you had intended to use. So we would caution you, don't forge ahead with your planning until you know what resources are available.

Generally the school will hold an inventory of the software that it possesses and in some schools this may even be linked to particular key stages or even units of work. It is worthwhile obtaining a copy of this inventory as soon as possible, as this will give you time to become acquainted with the products and their functionality. Ideally you would then be able to spend time in school, using each item in turn with a view to establishing its relevance and its potential usefulness for the teaching you are assigned. However, time is often short on an initial or pre-liminary visit and you may only have time to make notes or photocopies of the school's own documentation. A good impression can then be gained from the manufacturer's website, for it is in the manufacturer's interest to give an honest account of the uses to which a piece of software can be put. You may also then refer to websites such as the Schoolzone site cited above.

PRACTICAL TASK PRACTICAL TASK **PRACTICAL TASK** PRACTICAL TASK **PRACTICAL TASK**

Imagine the three products below appear in the school inventory:

*   **SUMS-KS2-Shape and Space;**
*   **Textease Timeline;**
*   **RM Early Years Windowbox.**

Use Google or any other search engine to conduct a general investigation of each title. While doing so, pay particular attention to the role and background of the people who have written the evaluations or descriptions. Consider which are the most useful to you and what mental 'filters' you need to employ in order to get a balanced and comprehensive idea of how the software works and how it can be applied. This activity should take you about 10 minutes in total and it would be worthwhile if you were to perform the same kind of investigation on the inventory you obtain from your placement school.

Does the software match the needs of the curriculum and of the children?

This question provides the link between the first two questions and is the key to making effective decisions about what resources will best support your teaching. It is important that once you are at the stage of considering which software to use, you do so in a rigorous and systematic way. Manufacturers, quite correctly, attempt to produce software that is visually satisfying and engagingly interactive. This is to ensure that the product is as appealing as possible to the user. However, it is just as important that you verify its utility as a teaching tool and satisfy yourself that it provides an effective way to achieve specific learning objectives.

There is no inherent tension between these agendas and software manufacturers conduct earnest and effective research into the needs of their clients, i.e. you and the children in your class. However, for any given lesson and any stage within that lesson you will need to ask yourself whether the software in question is the most effective and whether using that software is the most effective choice given the availability of other approaches. As this is essentially the bulk of the evaluation process, it can de divided further into subsidiary questions.

How easy is the software to use within the time and resources I have available?

This will be a big consideration. Most software is easy and intuitive to use. This is the basis of modern computer operating systems. However, some do take a little extra time to become fully acquainted with. It is important when you are teaching with the IWB that you are composed and in full control of the technology. On a short, busy placement you may not have the time to become fully familiar with the software. If you think that this is the case it may be best to avoid using that item altogether.

It may also be that the software requires items of additional equipment, or newer, more powerful computers than are available to you. It is important that you check these factors fully before you begin to use the equipment and the software in front of the children. Failing to do so could result in a badly delivered lesson.

In order to verify usability you must practise using the actual equipment. Practising on the computer at home or on a laptop in the staffroom is valuable, but it is vital that you rehearse your activities using the IWB in the classroom. If you are unfamiliar with the equipment or the software then it would also be worthwhile asking a fellow student to observe you without the children's presence, for it is not enough to be competent; you must develop a high level of confidence as well.

How will I have to teach using this software?

You should attempt to find software that fits in naturally with your style of teaching. However, for the reasons noted above it is not always easy to do so. To that end you need to be clear about how the software is best used, for not every piece of software is appropriate for use with an IWB. Even those that are compatible for one kind of IWB activity may not suit all approaches. For example, one piece of software may come into its own when used by small groups of children gathered around the IWB. If this is the case, trying to use it as a teaching tool may detract from the effectiveness of your teaching rather than enhancing it. Conversely, it may be the case that a piece of software is ideally suited to an exposition-based style of teaching, but is quite complicated for the children to use with any degree of independence.

Also consider how the features and characteristics of the software will have to be adapted to your own teaching needs and style. Again, this is best done through a careful process of investigation and rehearsal using the software and equipment. We have noticed that trainees will often attempt to use the whole of a piece of software rather than merely selecting the aspects that most suit the needs of the situation. We would urge you to consider which parts you need and use only these. The following classroom story gives an illustration of how this can be possible. The story relates to an online resource found at **www.headlinehistory.co.uk**. It may be worthwhile spending a little time exploring this site before reading the story; however, this is not completely necessary.

CLASSROOM STORY **CLASSROOM** STORY **CLASSROOM** STORY **CLASSROOM STORY**

David is a trainee on a graduate teacher programme (GTP) in a Year 3 class in a school in a rural area of the East Midlands. He has been asked to teach the QCA History Unit 9 – 'What Was it Like for Children in the Second World War?', www.standards.dfes.gov.uk/schemes2/history/his9/?view=get.

Many of the children have little concept of life in contexts other than small rural towns and villages. He intends to use an investigative approach to his history teaching, hopefully by getting his class to conduct interviews with his own grandparents, who were evacuated from Manchester at the outset of the Second World War. He found that he has difficulty encouraging the children to identify with the sense of dislocation and strangeness that urban evacuees experienced in rural communities.

He had also recently asked the school caretaker's father (who was 10 in 1940 and had attended that same school) to describe the experience of accommodating evacuees in his community. David learned the importance of establishing a base level of understanding and how that enabled the children to focus their questions and to develop their comprehension further. He is determined that the children will have this understanding in order to bring the later interview to life. The school is well resourced with artefacts, facsimile documents and ICT equipment, including IWBs. He decides to make the most of the resources available.

Using the software provided with the IWB, he prepares a number of slides. These feature the main questions and the key objectives for the session. He begins by showing images of Manchester, family life and the school, prior to the war. He has also scanned a number of artefacts and images and pasted them into slides. These include a name tag, a list of evacuees to the village, facsimile letters and archive photographs.

As each slide appears he uses focused questioning to elicit responses from the children relating to the image and the experience of the children depicted. As this aspect of the session closes he presents the children with the follow-up task. They are to write and illustrate a short piece based on the recorded interview with an evacuee.

He then opens a website that has been lying dormant, waiting at a page that can be found using the following pathway on the Headline History website, www.headlinehistory.co.uk. **Start Here > East Midlands > World War Two > Skill Level: Trainee Journalist > Children Flee Big Cities > Interview Witnesses > Girl. If you prefer, you can obtain a general impression from Figure 6.1.**

Figure 6.1. A screenshot from the BAFTA-winning website Headline History, produced by Associated Northcliffe Digital and commissioned by Culture Online, part of the DCMS

David then reminds the children of the task and plays the recorded interviews. Once these interviews have been watched and discussed, he returns to the IWB using the presentation software to begin to create a written word bank with the children. This word bank is then printed out and photocopied as a starting point for when the class resumes after the break. The differentiation for the task involved some children individually accessing the website through the classroom computers, while another group used the IWB to discuss and work through the next phase of the activity under the supervision of a teaching assistant.

This classroom example illustrates a key element in the effective use of the IWB, which is to combine resources – whatever their source. Just as you would expect to tailor a traditionally delivered session to the individuals in your class, you should also expect to adopt a similar approach to using a range of IWB resources.

What are the implications for differentiation and accessibility?

This question will be particularly pertinent if you intend the children in your class to use the IWB in groups or individually. There are also a number of issues concerning accessibility that are worth considering at this point.

Differentiation

As a matter of course you should aim to ensure that your work with the children is properly differentiated. As noted previously, commercial software necessarily tends towards the mid-point of ability. You should ensure that the resource that you elect to use has sufficient flexibility to be adapted to meet the needs of the groups and individuals in your class. A good example of an easily differentiated interactive teaching program (ITP) can be found on the DfES Standards site, **www.standards.dfes.gov.uk/primary/teachingresources/mathematics/ nns_itps/itp_difference/difference_1_2.swf**

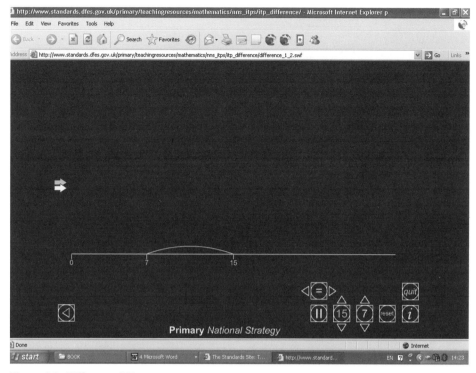

Figure 6.2. Difference ITP

This is the 'Difference ITP', which was released by the DfES in 2004 (see Figure 6.2). The teacher is given the option of choosing the range of numbers that the children can use. By restricting this and controlling the options presented to the children, the teacher can use this ITP in a way that is easily differentiated to the children's own needs.

Access

There are a number of access issues associated with the use of the IWB. These can tend to centre on the children's capacity to see and interpret what is written on the board. In terms of special educational needs provision, the child's individual education plan (IEP) will influence how the IWB is adapted for use with the child and the class. We will give two examples which will show the potential for customising the board to meet individual needs.

Though the causes of dyslexia are complex and to some extent unclear, there is some agreement that the colour of the background to the text has an impact upon the capacity of children to read the print. Blue is a favoured colour and children can be provided with blue eye filters to view text through or blue translucent glasses to support their reading. If a child has an IEP which requires that he or she is provided with such equipment then you are arguably not required to make further provision. However, for the benefit of children with undiagnosed requirements, or on the assumption that it could have a less pronounced but nevertheless tangible benefit for all children in the class, you can incorporate such research into the way you design your presentation. All IWBs have features that allow the teacher to choose the background to suit a task. One can also quickly replace a blank background with one containing lines or grids or a range of other patterns that may support SEN. For the purposes of contrast you can also change the font and the colour of text and research suggests that Comic Sans is a readable font that most children find attractive. To find out more about this and related questions, visit **www.bdadyslexia.org.uk/extra352.html**

If a child is visually impaired it is possible to use the accessibility functions available with Windows-based PCs to create an individual screen that is adapted for a specific child. These features are available from the Windows Control Panel and named Accessibility Options. You may not normally consider the use of these features to support differentiation, but when we are dealing with presenting ideas to children they lend themselves well to this aspect of your work.

It is also possible to create customised toolbars which use large icons. These are particularly useful if you need to adapt proprietary Windows-based software to the needs of individual children or groups. The following activity will demonstrate this.

PRACTICAL TASK PRACTICAL TASK **PRACTICAL TASK** PRACTICAL TASK **PRACTICAL TASK**

You have a child in your class who will need a customised toolbar in order for her to complete a group task on the IWB. This activity will demonstrate how to customise a toolbar in preparation.

1. Start by right-clicking on the grey area of the toolbar. You will see a drop-down menu featuring the names of the various toolbars available to the user (see Figure 6.3). The visible toolbars have a tick next to them and you can make others visible by clicking their entries on the list. To remove a visible toolbar, simply click the entry again.

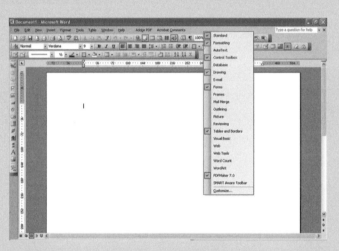

Figure 6.3. The complete list of available toolbars in MS Word

(Microsoft product screen shot reprinted with permission of Microsoft Corporation).

2. It is also possible to add buttons to or remove them from toolbars. This is done through the 'Customise' option, which follows the list of toolbars on the pop-up menu described above. From the Customise dialogue box (depicted in Figure 6.4), you can click the Commands tab, select the required toolbar from the Categories box and then drag desired tools onto the toolbar from the adjacent list of commands. To remove icons, click 'Rearrange commands', select the radio button next to 'Toolbar' and then 'Delete' icons from selected toolbars as required.

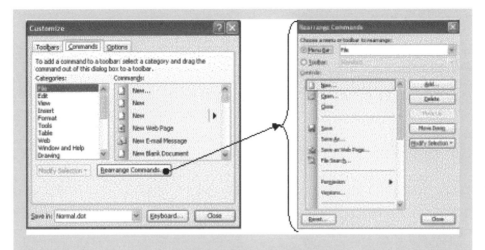

Figure 6.4. The Customise toolbar dialogue box with Rearrange Commands window
(Microsoft product screen shot reprinted with permission of Microsoft Corporation.)

3. You should now be able to control how the existing toolbars look and feel. Importantly, you can reduce the number of icons on a toolbar and then, from the Customise dialogue box (Figure 6.4) click on the Options tab and select 'Large icons', making key commands more visible.

4. Alternatively, create an entirely new toolbar by going to the Customise box. Select the Toolbars tab and then click the 'New' button. You will then see another box which allows you to choose the name for this menu (Figure 6.5).

Figure 6.5. The New Toolbar dialogue box

This toolbar will now appear on the list of toolbars and the precise buttons that are needed can be added to it as discussed in stage 1. You can also follow the instructions in stage 3 in order to increase the size of the icons. An example is provided in Figure 6.6 and you will be able to appreciate how, being larger, the icons are more easily distinguished from one another. By virtue of their being fewer in number, a child would find it easier to remember their specific functions.

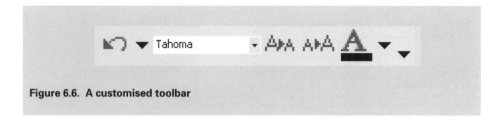

Figure 6.6. A customised toolbar

How will the children react to the software?

You also need to consider the way in which children will react to the ITP or the software that you are presenting them with. It is assumed that children will be motivated by the use of technology, but although the software and the interactive activity may be both engaging and motivating this must not distract the children in your class from the main objective. This is a critical balance, for the enthusiasm of the children for the resources must go beyond the spectacle of the IWB and extend to the core learning activity.

PRACTICAL TASK PRACTICAL TASK PRACTICAL TASK PRACTICAL TASK PRACTICAL TASK

Evaluating software

We have discussed a number of factors that can impact on your evaluation of software tools and teaching resources. This applies to purchased resources, ones that you have discovered on the internet and ones that you have created for yourself. As you grow in experience you will find that you begin to incorporate these considerations intuitively. This activity is designed to allow you to begin to develop this skill.

Spend a little time browsing www.iwb.org.uk and look for a resource that would fit in within an area that you have experienced, preferably in the role of trainee. If this is not possible, consider it in the context of a lesson that you have observed. Use the template provided below to guide your evaluation of the resource that you are examining.

Year:	Subject:	Theme
Lesson objective:		
Resource title:		
Title obtained from:		
What curriculum do I have to deliver?		
Does the software match the needs of the curriculum and of the children?		
How easy is the software to use within the time and resources I have available?		
How will I have to teach using this software?		

Year:		Subject:	Theme
What are the implications for differentiation and accessibility?			
What are the hardware issues?			
How will the children react to the software?			
Overall evaluation			

Commercially produced software and IWBs

There are some commercially produced software titles that are particularly effective for making learning objects and it is worth looking at some of these here.

Mind-mapping software and IWBs

With the increased awareness of varying learning styles and the growing popularity of a multi-sensory approach to teaching in the primary classroom, there has been an increase in the availability of child-friendly software that caters for visual learning techniques. In particular, there has been the development of software that supports the use of teaching strategies like mind-mapping. This is where ideas are graphically mapped out in a web-like format that makes use of arrowed links to show how ideas connect and relate to each other. Mind-mapping has been especially championed by Smith and Call in their popular publication *ALPS: Accelerated Learning in Primary Schools* (2000). They suggest that a visual representation of ideas helps the brain generate structure, understand relationships and organise and interpret ideas. Mind-mapping, a term originally coined by Buzan (1991), is often associated with accompanying vocabulary like 'brainstorming', 'ideas maps' and 'concept maps'.

Commercial software that allows for a visual representation of ideas can be used very effectively in conjunction with an IWB. Applications like 'Inspiration' or its child-friendly version, 'Kidspiration', are given an added dimension when blown up on a big screen that enables whole-class participation. Brainstormed ideas that are organised graphically in a visual map can be built up in a collaborative manner that involves the whole class. Kidspiration, an already effective piece of software on a PC, is given the 'wow' factor when used on an IWB. The opportunity for children to come to the board and physically add and manipulate their own links, while discussing their decisions with their peers, adds value to many learning scenarios.

Promethean Symbol/SMART Board™ Symbol

A feature of the ACTIV™ software that you should be aware of when using Kidspiration with Promethean software is the usefulness of the text-recognition feature. This allows for hand-written annotations to be automatically converted to typeface. This facility is also effective with a variety of hand-drawn shapes which will be recognised and turned in to precise symbols. The ink-aware tools allow you to achieve a similar effect on the SMART Board™ too.

Simulation software

Another extremely powerful piece of software is that which allows children to simulate role-playing scenarios in different contexts via simple animations, storyboarding and comic-strip exercises. Software like Kar2ouche allows children to animate objects, sequence events and create characters that speak and change position in order to create episodes of interest. Immersive Education, the producers of Kar2ouche, have developed many different titles to cater for numerous curricular subjects, including such diverse examples as 'The Vikings', 'Primary Shakespeare', 'Understanding Religion' and 'Social Communication'.

A tremendously useful attribute of the software is that it involves primary aged children in multimedia authoring in a manner that has not really been available until now as it proved too complex. Kar2ouche is complemented when used in conjunction with an IWB. Children can make scenes during a lesson that cry out to be shared with the rest of the class. To place work on a big screen in order to show to the rest of the class is a satisfying end to a lesson, while developing the storyboards on the IWB allows larger groups to collaborate than is possible in individual workstations. Peers can then become involved in evaluating the work, suggesting improvements while also celebrating achievements, which all help to raise the status and importance of the learning situation. Each piece of software also comes with ready-made files that can be shown on the IWB as lesson starters and stimulators for discussion.

A SUMMARY OF KEY POINTS

As a result of reading this chapter you should now be able to:

> choose and evaluate IWB resources;
> identify ways in which these resources can be adapted into your lessons;
> relate ideas and activities from different areas of the book;
> identify ways in which the IWB can be used to support differentiation.

Recommended websites

www.curriculumonline.gov.uk
Resources and their evaluation

www.google.co.uk
Search engine

www.headlinehistory.co.uk
Free history resources and animations

www.schoolzone.co.uk
50,000 free resources and evaluations

www.standards.dfes.gov.uk
DfES standards site, downloadable schemes of work and resources

7

Software, tools and applications

By the end of this chapter you should:

- understand how Word can be best used with an IWB;
- know how to make your own interactive teaching programs (ITPs) using PowerPoint and Excel;
- continue to further your understanding of how to use the IWB software to make your own ITPs.

Professional Standards for QTS

This chapter addresses the following Professional Standards for QTS:

Q7, Q17, Q23, Q25

Introduction

Although there are numerous ready-made resources available for use with an IWB, there will be occasions when it is necessary for you to make your own materials. As you become more confident in producing interactive resources, you will find yourself resorting to ready-made materials less frequently as your own will inevitably address your own requirements more precisely. Producing your own resources does not have to be a time-consuming business and with practice you will find that you begin to design for interactivity as a matter of course. This chapter aims to support the development of the skills you need to create interactive resources, with the software that comes with your IWB and common Windows applications.

Using Microsoft Word with an IWB

If you are new to using an IWB a good way to become more confident is to experiment by using a familiar application like Microsoft Word. For example, it is possible to work in MS Word on your IWB, where you can manipulate an existing document in a variety of ways. Remember you can use the board as a mouse and therefore select text, change the font size, highlight sections and so on. If you want to be able to move text then you will need to anticipate this when you create your document, inserting text into text boxes, for example, so that it can be moved about freely.

Both the SMART™ and ACTIV™ boards allow you to annotate over the top of Windows applications and if you are using the text-recognition tool on the ACTIVboard™ you will be able to manipulate those annotations in a reasonably flexible way. However, it is important to remember that you are not editing the Word document when you do so; you are merely working over the top of it.

If you are working on a SMART Board™, those annotations will be quite unstable, but you should notice that Windows applications, such as MS Word, have some added icons on the standard toolbar. These are depicted below and relate to a tool called Ink Aware. This allows you to work within the application itself, effectively editing that document in ways that can be saved in the normal MS Word format.

Starting from the left-hand side, the first tool allows you to save your annotations directly into your Word document as an image. When you open the document at a later date the original annotations will also be retrieved. If the next tool is selected, the Word application will attempt to translate anything that you write into editable text. To use this tool, place your cursor in the location that you want to insert the text and depress the icon. You may then begin to write on the board. The final Ink Aware tool should look familiar to you. When you click the camera icon, the content area of the current Word document will be captured and inserted as a new slide within a SMART™ Notebook file (SMART™ Technologies, 2006).

Regardless of the approach you use, there are some important issues that you need to be aware of when using a Windows application on an IWB.

- You must ensure that the text is rendered in a way that can be seen by all, which generally requires you to use a larger point size than the 12 points that you would use for printing. However, instead of changing the font size you might elect to increase the percentage view from 100% to 150% – this tool can be found as an optional drop-down menu located on the top toolbar.

- The toolbars in most Windows application are located at the top of the screen, as close as possible to eye level for the normal computer user. The top of the screen is actually the least accessible region of an IWB so you may want to move them to a more easily reachable location. To do this move the cursor to the far left-hand side of the toolbar that you wish to move, where you will see four vertically arranged black dots. As you move the cursor across the dots it will turn into a four-way arrow, indicating that an object can be moved. You can then click and drag the toolbar to the bottom of the application window. To customise your toolbar further, refer to Chapter 6 and the section entitled 'Access'.

Of course anything that you find in Word can be copied into the SMART Notebook™ application, or into the ACTIV™ flipchart. However, there are a number of instances when you may not want to do this. Applications like MS Word or Mariner have their own strengths and if you want to try these you will need to acquire the skills that will allow you to use them effectively on your IWB.

PRACTICAL TASK PRACTICAL TASK **PRACTICAL TASK** PRACTICAL TASK **PRACTICAL TASK**

- **Create a document in your preferred word-processing application by typing or pasting a short block of text.**
- **Remove all verbs and adjectives and place each one in a text box, leaving an amount of white space in their place sufficient for them to be replaced later.**
- **Rehearse an activity on your whiteboard where you restore the missing words to their places**
- **Annotate the text, labelling the different 'parts of speech'. Use the text recognition facility to change your annotations into typescript.**

Composing writing

The IWB can be used to great effect when creating a class composition, and has a particularly important role to play in promoting visual literacy. The IWB supports a more collaborative approach to writing because it displays text in an accessible way and allows it to be reorganised and annotated in a very immediate and dynamic fashion. You can also introduce various kinds of visual and audible stimuli and can support the various processes involved in literary composition. For example, an image can be displayed and short descriptive phrases can be superimposed upon it. The image can then be reduced in size or removed completely, providing space for the vocabulary and phrases that it inspired to be organised into a narrative structure.

CLASSROOM STORY **CLASSROOM** STORY **CLASSROOM** STORY **CLASSROOM STORY**

Jennifer is a student teacher who wants to develop descriptive writing, emphasising the use of adjectives. Jennifer was working with a large Year 4 class and their topic for the term was 'The Seashore', which she was exploring in conjunction with the objectives from the National Literary Strategy. Jennifer wished to stimulate the children's imagination and promote a classroom discussion exploring 'describing words'. As part of her lesson preparation she looked on 'Google Image' (http://images.google.co.uk/) to search for stormy pictures as a starting point for the writing. Having found a suitable picture of a storm, with the sea lashing a ship, she copied and pasted it into a Word document. Jennifer checked for any apparent copyright issues before displaying the image and then used the IWB's 'Spotlight' tool so that only one part of the picture could be seen.

During the lesson, initially the children could only see a fragment of the picture. This helped create a sense of mystery and intrigue as to what the picture might be about and provoked initial discussion over what story it might tell. Gradually, as Jennifer revealed the whole picture, by increasing the size of the spotlight, she tried to get the children to write down words to describe it on their own individual mini-whiteboards. The class then fed back their suggestions and the teacher made a bank of adjectives on the IWB.

At this point Jennifer opened another Word document and used the 'Restore Down/Maximise' icon in order to adjust the size of the window in each Word document so that they sat side by side on the desktop. This enabled the children to see the storm stimulus and word bank while placing their adjectives into sentences on the other half of the screen.

Jennifer then progressed to the next part of the lesson by formulating some shared writing. She and the children used a wireless keyboard that was passed around the class in order to produce a number of descriptive sentences about the storm using the adjectives suggested in the previously made word bank. The class then discussed how the order of the sentences could enhance the impact of the writing as a whole. The children then came to the board to highlight particular sentences and move them so that the text read smoothly and with increasing dramatic effect that mirrored the progress of a storm.

> **REFLECTIVE** TASK
> REFLECTIVE TASK
>
> Consider what benefits the use of an IWB has in this classroom story.

> **PRACTICAL TASK** PRACTICAL TASK PRACTICAL TASK PRACTICAL TASK PRACTICAL TASK
>
> • **Open a new file using SMART Notebook or ACTIVprimary software.**
> • **Go to Google Image** (http://images.google.co.uk/) **and search for a suitable storm scene that you might use with a class.**
> • **Copy and paste your chosen image into a slide or flipchart page.**
>   **Locate the Spotlight tool and experiment with applying it to the picture.**
> • **Explore the different shapes the spotlight can make and use it to highlight different parts of the scene you have elected to use. Find out how to close the Spotlight tool once you have finished with it. (Refer to Chapter 1 if required.)**

Using Microsoft PowerPoint with an IWB

PowerPoint contains design features that augment its usefulness when used on an IWB. While the software is operating in design mode the Ink Aware features on the SMART Board™ can be used to input content directly onto slides using the pen tools. In mouse mode, both SMART™ and ACTIV™ boards can be used in lieu of the mouse to introduce, organise and manipulate objects. However, in addition to this the IWB software allows the user to input content into a presentation while it is being delivered in display mode as well. This is achieved in the following way:

• **Open a PowerPoint file and annotate the information while the program is in Slide Show mode (as opposed to Edit mode).**
• **Select the menu button in the Slide Show toolbar (a rectangular icon located in between two arrow icons).**
• **Select 'Save Annotations to PowerPoint'. Any annotation will subsequently become a permanent part of the PowerPoint file.**

Teaching with PowerPoint on an IWB

PowerPoint offers the facility to make presentations dynamic as it is very easy to add multimedia effects like clip art, photographs, sound and movies. The ability to integrate audio content and moving images is particularly valuable as these are not easily integrated with the software that comes with the IWB. PowerPoint also offers some particularly good features that support effective and interactive teaching, but many PowerPoint presentations that you have seen will doubtless have failed to exploit them. This is largely because of the context in which they are used – during the delivery of a conference paper perhaps – where opportunities for interaction are limited. The following discussion focuses on facilities that are appropriate for classroom contexts and work with children, facilities that can be brought to life using an IWB. What follows is a discussion of some of the more interactive ways that PowerPoint can be used to create enjoyable lessons and to enhance learning opportunities.

Using animation to model concepts

PowerPoint offers useful and simple animation tools and the so-called 'motion paths' can be used to good effect in conjunction with an IWB. Although this application does not have anywhere near the power of a true animation package like Macromedia Flash, which offers far more powerful content authoring tools, PowerPoint benefits from having a more manageable range of features that are easy to navigate and do not require the user to grapple with any type of programming language. Indeed, its tools are so simple that older primary aged children can use and understand them with ease. From your perspective as a teacher, animations allow you to automate demonstrations of a concept in a fashion that might otherwise be difficult to achieve.

CLASSROOM STORY **CLASSROOM** STORY **CLASSROOM** STORY **CLASSROOM STORY**

Student teacher Jason was finding it hard to teach the concept of pluralisation to his class. He therefore decided to try a more visual approach by using PowerPoint in conjunction with the IWB. To show how singular words could be converted to their plural versions, he formulated a PowerPoint slide show that contained the pluralisation rules. To make the slide show more stimulating, he inserted motion paths to 'model' the rules the children had to learn. For instance, when converting the singular 'lady' to the plural 'ladies' he typed the word 'lady' on the screen and then inserted a motion path so that when the children touched the word on the IWB the 'y' would magically 'move' from the screen and the 'ies' would 'fly' in and take its place. So that he wasn't reliant on clicking the mouse to activate the motion path animation, he set the animation to run in response to a 'trigger'; the trigger in this case was a click (or tap) on the text object 'LAD' (Figure 7.1).

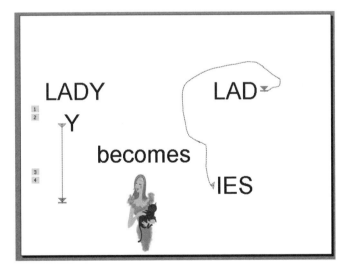

Figure 7.1. Movement paths an example of a child's Powerpoint slide show to show pluralisation rule

Alongside this activity Jason verbalised the rule for words ending in 'y' that are preceded by a consonant with 'drop the "y" and add "ies"', and similar motion paths were included for the exemplification of other pluralisation rules.

While it is not the IWB offering the special effects here, and the use of motion paths has been a common feature in PowerPoint for several years, it is the combination of technologies that now makes this type of animation so effective. The IWB allows for the whole class to view and indeed trigger the animation with ease and this in turn promotes collaboration. By adding alternative endings with their own motion paths and by resetting the triggers so that they were associated with the endings themselves, rather than the root of the word, the presentation could be made even more interactive, giving the user a choice of correct and incorrect solutions. This would allow another level of exploration and discussion to take place.

Jason progressed the lesson by challenging the children to make their own PowerPoint files, demonstrating the pluralisation spelling rule on nouns of their choice. He taught them how to insert a motion path so that they could animate their presentations and allowed 50 minutes for the task. As a plenary activity the children showed each other their PowerPoint slide shows on the IWB. The children presented their work, explaining the rules, and invited their peers to come to the board to trigger the motion path effects.

This lesson may sound complex, but children who are familiar with PowerPoint can handle motion paths and triggers with ease. They enjoy experimenting with techniques like these and this sort of activity can make the learning of sterile spelling rules much more inspiring. Having the rest of the class viewing and testing their work on the IWB provides further motivation to achieve.

To insert a motion path in your own PowerPoint file:

- **select the object you wish to animate;**
- **from the toolbar select Slide Show > Custom Animation;**
- **from the panel that appears (usually on the right of the screen) select Add Effect > Motion Path. A variety of different motion paths can be chosen but the option 'Draw Custom Path' offers the most flexibility;**
- **to set the trigger, right-click on the animation you have just created in the list of custom animations and select 'Timing';**
- **click the button labelled 'Trigger' and choose the object that will activate the animation.**

Action buttons and multi-path presentations

Action buttons are another valuable tool to use when making learning resources. Action buttons allow a PowerPoint file to move from a mere linear display of information to being able to give a child an element of choice. This allows him or her to follow multiple paths in the presentation, thereby making it a more diverse experience. This is a crucial element which allows a child to interact with a program. It lets a child explore and ask those vital 'what if' questions by experimenting with different lines of enquiry. By the careful addition of action buttons, presentations become more challenging and thought-provoking. Action buttons can be created as follows.

- **Select 'Slide Show' from the toolbar at the top of the screen.**
- **Then select 'Action Buttons' from the subsequent drop-down menu.**
- **Select a suitable button from the available options.**
- **Place your cursor in the desired location on screen, depress the left mouse button and drag. This last operation 'draws' the button and determines its size. On releasing the mouse button, a menu will appear, which lets you specify where the action button will take the user when it is selected.**
- **Indicate how you wish to activate the button by selecting the tab 'Mouse Click' or 'Mouse Over'.**
- **Choose the option 'Hyperlink to' and select from the drop-down window the chosen destination of the button.**

CLASSROOM STORY **CLASSROOM** STORY **CLASSROOM** STORY **CLASSROOM STORY**

Student teacher Charlotte was investigating writing stories, particularly concentrating on exploring the element of the inclusion of 'dilemmas' in story situations. Having read and discussed several stories, she then showed the class an interactive book she had produced using PowerPoint. Charlotte had taken the traditional fairy tale of Goldilocks and used clip art, animation, text and audio clips to retell the story. Action buttons were included for the children to be able to progress from one page to the next. However, Charlotte also added action buttons to give a multi-path dimension to the story. At critical points the children were able to choose the course of action for Goldilocks and to dictate the outcome of the tale. The children could then follow various paths to experience two very different outcomes to the story. For instance, when Goldilocks was hungry the class had to decide whether or not she should eat the porridge on offer; the PowerPoint file then travelled in two different directions to reveal different story outcomes related to the option chosen.

The PowerPoint book was shown via the IWB. This allowed the children to take control of the presentation and manipulate the action buttons to investigate different scenarios. This approach demonstrated very well the structure of a story, dilemma and resolutions. It also invited much class involvement in the form of direct interaction and through the collaboration and discussion that surrounded the various choices that the children had to make.

Again, as with motion paths, the inclusion of action buttons is not a new idea but when used with the addition of IWB technology they can provide some very effective learning scenarios that allow the children to control much of the action.

It is quite within the capabilities of older junior children to make their own interactive stories utilising a multi-path dimension via PowerPoint's action buttons. Their final books can be presented on the IWB to their peers or can be made with a younger audience in mind so that they could be shown to the younger year groups in the school.

Using PowerPoint and IWBs with early years children

It might be thought that PowerPoint is too complex an application to use with early years children. However, the following classroom story will highlight how to effectively utilise PowerPoint with an IWB when working with the Foundation Stage.

The combination of PowerPoint and an IWB make for an effective duo here. It is very easy to add sound files, which is not easily achieved in bespoke IWB applications, and insert photographs into PowerPoint. The IWB provides a platform where more than one child can work on the photos to allow for collaboration and increased interactivity is also provided by the IWB as it allows the children to easily manipulate the photographs. The technology helps young children to sequence events and develop chronological understanding. The use of Windows Sound Recorder makes it easy to record their own interpretation and narration of the day without involving the effort of writing, which can interrupt a child's train of thought at this stage. Appropriate application can then be given to the inclusion of accurate captions for the photographs, which acts as a more realistic writing task at this level.

A Reception class had recently visited a local supermarket as part of their termly topic on 'Where We Live'. The class teacher and accompanying student teacher, Kim, had taken digital cameras on the trip. The children had all been involved in taking pictures of various sections of the supermarket and of their trip on the bus that took them to and from the shop.

On their return to school, Kim uploaded the pictures and placed a selection of them on a PowerPoint slide. Working in small groups with the support of Kim, the children were shown the PowerPoint file on the IWB. The children were then asked to select the photographs and drag them so that that the pictures were placed in the right chronological order to show how the day progressed. Instead of the children having the cumbersome task of trying to type phrases about the photographs, Kim set up the microphone on the PC and used Windows Sound Recorder so that the children could record themselves explaining each picture. When the children were happy with the recordings Kim saved the files and inserted them into the PowerPoint presentation. The children then positioned the file under its relevant picture. The children completed the exercise by giving each picture a one-word title. They then decided whether they wished to type or use the IWB pens to annotate their work.

Windows Sound Recorder can be located by selecting:

- Start > Programs > Accessories > Entertainment > Sound Recorder

Using Microsoft Excel to make ITPs to use with an IWB

The application Excel can be manipulated in order to produce your own interactive teaching programs. Formulas can be created that appear to make your applications intelligent and are particularly useful when making your own mathematical 'games'. There are plenty of free ITPs available that can be used to enhance numeracy teaching, as discussed in Chapter 6. However, there may just be some occasions when you cannot find a program to meet a specific learning objective and you need to be able to make your own material.

Student teacher Leah wanted to consolidate her teaching of subtraction in an open-ended manner that incorporated a problem-solving dimension. Leah was working in a mixed key stage class of Years 2 and 3 who had a wide range of abilities and needs. Having perused many ready-made ITPs she could not find any materials that would suit the particular needs of the children. She therefore decided to use Excel to make her own ITP.

Leah made the 'spreadsheet' image that appears in Excel more child-friendly by selecting a large area of cells and using the 'fill' tool to add a pale green background. She then used Word Art to produce a title, borders to give individual cells definition and text boxes, auto shapes or call-outs, to contain any necessary instructions. The file was then made to work out any required calculations by the use of a simple formula using an 'if' statement. For instance, in the case of the first number problem 30 – 14 on the screenshot image provided in Figure 7.2, the required statement would be:

=IF(F11=B5-D5,'WELL DONE','TRY AGAIN')

More sums were added by placing a similar formula in different locations and the file was shown on the IWB for all the class to view. A wireless keyboard was passed around so that the children could enter answers and receive immediate feedback with a 'Well Done' or 'Try Again'. Leah could use the program to meet the needs of the whole class by changing the initial target number – no change to the inserted formula was required to do this.

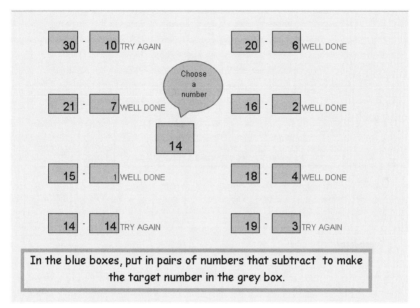

Figure 7.2. Excel subtraction game

Using IWB software to make ITPs

The software that accompanies your IWB – Notebook or ACTIVprimary™ – is the most adaptable tool to use when making ITPs. If you require children to do extensive dragging and dropping of objects in order to find solutions to problems, you will find they will do so more easily in the specialist IWB applications as they are designed with this activity in mind. The manipulation of objects, resizing images for example, can be fiddly in Windows applications which provide much smaller 'handles', suitable for use with a precision input device like the mouse. You will find that you can build presentations more flexibly as well.

CLASSROOM STORY **CLASSROOM** STORY CLASSROOM STORY **CLASSROOM STORY**

Student teacher Karen was teaching a Year 3/4 class about healthy eating and different food groups. She decided to use her IWB to produce an interactive scenario.

The lesson began by introducing the children to food groups and the concept of a healthy diet. To illustrate, Karen displayed on the IWB the food pyramid taken from the SMART Board gallery and discussed with the children why some sections were larger than others and the importance of eating less of some foods and more of others. The next two pages of Notebook displayed a food pyramid above the components of a meal and a drink, one healthy and one unhealthy. To promote interactivity, Karen invited children to drag and drop the food into the correct group on the SMART Board. The class then discussed if the meal was balanced, if any food group had been omitted from the meal and if most of the food was based in the largest sections of the pyramid. Working in pairs, the children then thought about and discussed the food they had eaten the previous day and completed their own food groups diagram on a pre-printed proforma, before feeding back their findings and discussing any surprises they had discovered about their own diets.

The children were then asked how drinks could increase their intake of fruit and vegetables and which drinks they considered would be the most effective.

A large collection of empty drinks' packaging, containing the nutritional information of a variety types of manufactured drinks, was then introduced. These ranged from pure fruit smoothies to squashes and the children investigated the contents of the drinks from the nutritional information provided by the manufacturer. The children were shown a bottle of orange squash and invited to predict the ingredients. To avoid any confusion, Karen modelled how to find the manufacturer's information. Using a label previously scanned into Notebook, Karen demonstrated where to find the ingredients list, how to find the greatest three ingredients and the nutritional information they would be comparing. The children were then provided with evaluation sheets for their investigations and from the scanned label Karen modelled how to complete the sheets on a copy displayed on the IWB.

The children chose from the large selection of packages and investigated the contents of at least four different drinks, completing an evaluation sheet for each package. At the end of the activity the class fed back their findings. Karen entered a number of the children's findings on the sheet displayed on the IWB and the fruit, sugar and calorific content of the drinks were discussed. The discussion led on to how some of the drinks could have been made healthier, and the children thought about how this may affect the taste of the drinks.

The extension task, which some children achieved, was to table and graph the findings using Microsoft Excel, which Karen initially modelled on the IWB.

PRACTICAL TASK PRACTICAL TASK **PRACTICAL TASK** PRACTICAL TASK **PRACTICAL TASK**

Part 1 Make your own resources using your IWB software.

- **Your first task is to make a simple Tudor timeline. By looking at the installed resources available on your board you might find a ready-made blank timeline. It is also easy to make your own timeline using the straight-line tool to make one horizontal line with small vertical markers attached along its length to signify important dates.**

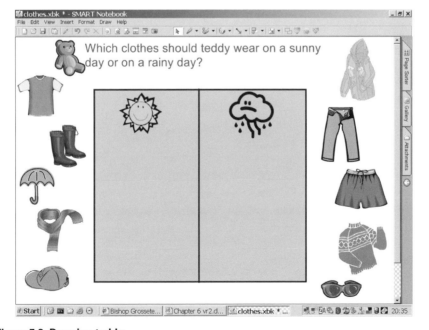

- Group and lock your timeline into place.
- You are now ready to populate your page with images of key events from the Tudor era. By using the IWB resource banks, or by finding appropriate images from the internet, place these pictures at the top or bottom of the page. You may like to place an accompanying date under the picture and group the image and date as one object that can be dragged by the children.

Part 2

It is the task of the children to drag the images into chronological order on the timeline. To aid the class in solving the problem you can include one last element on your page. Insert an image of a question mark or alternatively write the word 'help'. Now investigate how to turn this object into a hyperlink so that when it is clicked it will take the children to a web page that contains relevant information on key dates in the Tudor period.

CLASSROOM STORY **CLASSROOM** STORY **CLASSROOM** STORY **CLASSROOM STORY**

Student teacher Tooni was spending her final teaching placement with a Foundation Stage class. The class were exploring different types of clothes and equipment a person might need for different types of weather. Tooni created three whiteboard screens for the children to use. One screen contained a teddy on a hot day surrounded by a selection of warm-weather clothes. The children had to drag the clothes onto the teddy while discussing why these clothes were good for this sort of day. The second screen presented a similar exercise but the children had to dress teddy on a rainy day. The third screen required the children to make decisions and divide an assortment clothes into appropriate categories that might be seen on a hot or cold day. See Figure 7.3.

Figure 7.3. Dressing teddy

PRACTICAL TASK PRACTICAL TASK **PRACTICAL TASK** PRACTICAL TASK **PRACTICAL TASK**

Test your knowledge of an IWB. Try and make a sorting exercise similar to that presented above. Make an IWB resource that requires Foundation Stage children to classify domestic animals against those that might be found in the wild.

A SUMMARY OF **KEY POINTS**

As a result of reading this chapter you should:

> be aware of practical considerations when using Microsoft Word with an IWB;
> know some effective ways to use PowerPoint with an IWB;
> have an emerging understanding of how to make learning objects using Excel;
> show increasing independence when making resources using SMART Notebook™ or the ACTIVprimary™ software.

8

The online dimension

By the end of this chapter you should:

- search effectively for online resources;
- integrate the use of online resources with your use of the IWB;
- understand issues associated with the use of online resources in the classroom;
- adapt resources to meet your own needs;
- enable the children to create their own online resources to share with each other.

Professional Standards for QTS

This chapter addresses the following Professional Standards for QTS:

Q3.1.3, Q14, Q17, Q23, Q25

Introduction

The purpose of this chapter is to give you the opportunity to consider some of the options that you have in using the internet in conjunction with your use of the IWB. To some extent it is slightly misleading to have a separate chapter dedicated to this single aspect, as the use of the internet is now almost ubiquitous. With the growing use of broadband, the distinction between software held on the computer or on CD-ROM and that which forms part of an online resource is becoming less marked. This is a positive development, as it is becoming easier to access a wealth of online resources that can lend additional versatility to your teaching. In this chapter we hope to demonstrate how you can take advantage of this and enhance your teaching as a result.

The ideal situation

As a student teacher, you are setting out on your professional career at a time when your own competence with ICT and the skills possessed by the children in your class are of central importance to your effectiveness. Your experience of school placement is likely to vary according to the level of equipment in the classroom, but it is highly likely that it will involve interaction with technical hardware and a range of software tools. This chapter makes a number of assumptions regarding the equipment that you have access to and the ways in which you are able to work with it, but you should not judge any classroom against these assumptions. You may ultimately be in a position to influence the equipment of a school and you will doubtless see specific tools and specific technologies as having an important role to play in this process. However, underpinning the examples found here are much broader principles of ICT use that you should be able to apply immediately, regardless of the circumstances that you find yourself in. Ultimately it is not the usefulness of the tool itself, but your effectiveness as a teacher that will make the difference.

The first assumption is that there is an IWB and projector combination in the classroom. Ideally this should be configured so that you are able to use it with a computer that is connected to the internet via a broadband or other high-speed connection.

If you are able to connect to the internet in a wireless environment you will find yourself in a position to use laptop computers very flexibly. You could, for example, work with the children around the classroom and then bring the laptop back to a position where it could be connected to an IWB, without having to interrupt the activity or transfer data to another machine by some other means.

If you are not able to take advantage of a wireless internet connection, you will need to think about how to transport information and documents between computers that are used by the class and those that attach to IWBs. USB memory sticks are very useful for this purpose as they offer a very quick and easy way to transfer files. However, memory sticks are not as robust as people sometimes assume and you should not think of them as the best way of storing information for long periods of time.

Searching the internet

It is probable that you are already familiar with searching the internet using search engines such as Google (**www.google.co.uk**). Google is a 'crawler' or 'spider'-based search engine. This means that software automatically 'crawls' around the internet looking for content. Key words from this content are noted, as are URLs (Universal Resource Locator or internet addresses). These are then used to catalogue, or 'index', sites that are relevant to your search and have been visited by other internet users.

Google, as the most widely used search engine, is referred to in examples found throughout this chapter, as are some other specifically educationally focused alternatives. However, it is fair to say that much of what is said here could be applied generally and you might prefer to use other search engines. It is likely that you are familiar with the main screen of Google and though it looks very uncluttered and straightforward it offers a great deal more than can be appreciated at first inspection. While this simplicity means that it is easy to overlook some useful tools, it also means that once they are discovered they can be accessed very easily.

Localising your search

The main screen of Google gives you the opportunity to search either in the UK or on the internet as a whole. This is normally set to search the entire Web, but if you wanted to search for content that is related specifically to the UK then select the 'UK' radio button, which is located immediately below the main keyword entry box. If you are interested in isolating content from other countries, you could try entering the suffix appropriate to that country as a keyword in your search or alter the URL so that you go to the Google page for that country. For example, if you go to **www.google.fr** you will raise the French site and will receive the options to search only French websites or only websites that are written in the French language.

Go to www.google.cn and search for the 'Great Wall'. The China Tourism website for the Great Wall appears early in the list. Compare this with the list of results offered by the same search at www.google.co.uk, where there are a number of sites about the Great Wall.

Searching for still images

Google also offers an Image Search facility. Clicking the 'Images' link, located second in a horizontal list of options displayed just above the keyword entry box, will enable you to search for a range of images for inclusion in your presentations. These are taken from the whole of the World Wide Web, so an image search for 'Great Wall of China' on this screen will take you to a wide range of images of the Great Wall that can be used to support your teaching.

Inserting these images into your presentations is simply a matter of clicking the thumbnail of the image and then clicking the link that reads 'See full-sized image', which appears at the top of the screen that opens as a result. You can then either drag that image into Notepad, or cut and paste it into any other application.

At this point it is important to introduce a note of caution regarding the copyright of an image or other content. Copyright needs to be checked to ensure that it is not infringed by your intended use of it and it will often be necessary, or at the very least courteous, to request permission to use content that has been created or published by someone else. You should also take the time to credit the author of a piece of work that you use (more guidance is provided on this issue at the end of this chapter). As a general rule, if you haven't time or the patience for this, include terms like 'copyright free', 'free' or 'educational content' into your keyword search in order to identify useable content. You might also locate and keep a list of useful content providers such as **www.free-picture-graphic.org.uk/** for it is often better to use these rather than to attempt a search of unknown websites.

Incorporating online video

There is a wide range of online video content available for you to use in your presentations to the children. Perhaps the most famous of these is YouTube, which can be found at **www.youtube.com**, or by clicking the 'more' link on the Google home page. Considerable caution is required here, for it is never advisable to browse sites like this in the classroom. Much of the content placed on these sites is produced by individuals who have created the material themselves and are merely seeking an audience for it. There is also a considerable amount of content that is included in contravention of copyright regulations. Although these sites are regulated, there is inappropriate content here so the use of these sites by children must be very carefully regulated.

The videos can be included in your presentations in the following ways. Simply copying the URL of the video into your presentation is a simple method that often avoids copyright issues. However, this does mean that you will probably be confronted by banner or pop-up adverts of an unpredictable nature.

Google also offers a proprietary video player option. This lets you download video content into the player and allows you to play it in an application that is separate from the website itself. Once the link has been created to the video content, it will run reliably, providing the computer that you are using is connected to the internet. This window can be controlled and used in exactly the same way any other screen containing content. The only alternative is to download the video clip itself. This can involve storing quite large files on your computer, but there are three advantages to this approach. You can have your video clips stored in a folder and just double click on them in order to have them played by your default media player. You will need to wait for a considerably shorter period of time before the clips start to play and it is less likely that the playback will stall while the computer 'catches up'. Finally, you have complete control over what is displayed and you won't run the risk of finding that the website providing the content suddenly closes or suffers technical problems the moment you need the content.

Maps and other content

There is a range of other content available using advanced search engines such as that offered by Google. Perhaps one of the most impressive is the mapping and satellite imagery service offered. This provides views of most areas of the world at varying degrees of magnification and can provide maps or satellite photographs. A real strength of this is that Google also offers a 'Hybrid' version of the two, where a selected region of map is made semi-transparent and can be dragged across an aerial photograph of the same region. Multimap also offers a useful tool of this kind.

By using the Hybrid feature, for example, you will be able to relate what the children have already experienced with maps and their exploration of the local area to a combination of the two, which will give a clear impression of the way in which the map and actual landscape relate to each other. You can explore the different kinds of information that photographs and maps convey and what features of the landscape they do not reveal so well. Using an IWB you can conduct these explorations in a variety of different ways: incorporating different kinds of content, including that created in digital media by the children themselves, marking it up or annotating over the top as appropriate.

CLASSROOM STORY **CLASSROOM** STORY CLASSROOM STORY **CLASSROOM STORY**

Student teacher Neave was teaching her Year 5 class about special places during an RE lesson. The children had recently been on a trip to visit Lincoln Cathedral. At the start of the lesson Neave looked at the website of Lincoln Cathedral in order to refresh the children's memories of their recent day out. Upon entering the website Neave decided to access their virtual tour (http://www.lincolncathedral.com/tour). This tour initially shows a plan of the building and allows the audience to navigate where they wish to explore by selecting certain clickable hotspots. Children in the class where asked to come up to the interactive whiteboard and select where they wished to go. At this point Neave let the children use the board to determine the course of this part of the lesson. One child chose to explore "the font" while another decided to navigate to the cloister. At each destination the children were able to discuss what was special about each feature using information they had found out on the tour and supplementing it with textual facts found on the virtual tour. Neave discussed what sorts of features were common to all Christian buildings. She then accessed a webcam that showed pictures of a very simple church. Neave was then able to locate features such as the font and compare and contrast these with the font and other features seen in the cathedral.

Neave divided the children up into small, mixed ability groups of three. She gave each group a special place to investigate. Neave asked the children to investigate special places from different religions, for instance, some children were investigating mosques while others were exploring synagogues. During the main part of the lesson the children had to piece together a presentation detailing the main features that might be found in that building. Neave had prepared a selection of websites that contained suitable information for each special place to act as a starting point for the children. Some children were able to undertake supervised searches using a search tool like 'Google' (www.google.com). The children were able to cut and paste images of features of their special place to add to their presentation (copyright permitting). Some children also entered hyperlinks to web exemplars of their special place. A few proactive children located a webcam in the proximity of their special place. For instance, a group which was continuing to look at different Christian cathedrals located a webcam showing live images from outside Canterbury Cathedral.

At the end of the lesson the children presented their information on the interactive whiteboard. Groups which had inserted hyperlinks to other websites were able to show how their links worked and how they enhanced their presentation.

REFLECTIVE TASK

Why is an IWB important here? How does it bring more than a data projector and screen?

PRACTICAL TASK PRACTICAL TASK PRACTICAL TASK PRACTICAL TASK PRACTICAL TASK

The aim of this activity is to enable you to develop a focused approach to searching using the Advanced Search feature on Google. The purpose is to explore the most effective way of using the phrase 'free electronic whiteboard resources'. On the regular search, type this phrase into the search box and select 'the web' radio button. You should have about 920,000 sites in the list. Now try the same search by clicking the link for advanced search and entering the phrase into the top, which is labelled 'with all of the words'. There will still be a very large number of 'hits' so we will have to take an even more focused approach. Try to narrow it down by entering the keywords into other boxes. If you really must have free resources, then the word 'free' should be in the first box. Also if you are trying to find electronic whiteboard resources then the 'exact phrase' must appear in the appropriate box. However, if resources are the most important aspect then move the word 'electronic' to the 'with at least one word' and perhaps add the word 'interactive' to that box too. All the time that you are doing this, notice the effect that this has on the number of indicated hits. Some combinations yield as few as 10 hits, others produce thousands.

Now try this same activity to gather resources on the following areas.

- Free online history resources for Key Stage 2.
- Electronic whiteboard resources for early years mathematics.
- Electronic whiteboard resources to support the Early Learning Goals.

You can then adapt the activity to try to identify specific resources that could support you in your work in your placement school.

Advanced searching

Google offers the facility for advanced searching and it is useful to spend some time discussing this. Clicking on the link to 'Advanced Search' will invoke the advanced search screen, which contains a number of boxes for refined search criteria. For example, it indicates words to include and exclude, the language that the results must appear in and the type of file that the results should represent. These are largely self-explanatory and practised use will save you time, enabling you to adopt a much more focused approach to your searching. The following activity will help to develop this point.

Other internet sources

The above section is dedicated to discovering resources for yourself. This is often a time-consuming business, which can lead to a good deal of frustration. This is often due to the huge amount of data that has to be sifted in order to find something of value. As teachers and student teachers we are quite rightly keen to be as precise as possible in matching the resource to the objectives and the class. However, it is worth remembering that in earlier chapters we have examined the ways in which resources can be adapted to individual circumstances. If it is not possible to get an exact match then it should be possible to adapt the activity to make that resource more effective.

It is increasingly becoming acknowledged that 'packaged' teaching resources are not as easy to design in a way that makes them easily shareable as people had hoped, despite the existence of a national curriculum. Teachers have different approaches and different requirements. We are moving towards a situation where resources will be provided more at the level of building blocks, useful materials that can be combined to create working teaching resources. For the time being, however, you will need to be prepared to adapt more fully developed resources for yourself – do not expect to find something that you can just slot into your teaching.

With this in mind we will now look at resource banks that are available, free to use, on the internet. These resource banks are valuable as they offer easily accessible resources, which are often written by classroom professionals and are matched to the objectives and year groups that you will encounter in your teaching. Two of the most significant of these are the National Whiteboard Network and the Teacher Resource Exchange.

National Whiteboard Network

The National Whiteboard Network is a subset of the DfES Standards site. It is organised around curriculum areas and is then subdivided into the areas associated with the QCA Schemes of Work, which you are probably already familiar with. The National Whiteboard Network can be found at **www.nwnet.org.uk**. The site offers guides to effective practice for classroom teachers, school leaders and LEA managers. It is updated regularly and there is a high degree of match between current DfES policy and thinking and the resources on offer. This is positive as it helps identify common and consistent themes that you will encounter as part of your development, both in schools and in the university setting. The layout of the site is essentially hierarchical and you can either bring up lists of content relevant to the main curriculum areas that are listed just below the main banner, or use the links contained in the boxes in the centre of the page to focus in on specific age groups and key stages.

Teacher Resource Exchange

Turning to specific internet-based resources and sources we now look at the Teacher Resource Exchange (TRE). The TRE can be found at **http://tre.ngfl.gov.uk** and is a moderated database of resources created by and for the use of teachers. It is sponsored by Becta and as a result the resources are of high quality and relate directly to curriculum areas. As you will see, to get the full benefit of this website it is necessary to log on as a registered user, which is a simple process mediated by clear on-screen instructions. Once you are a registered user you will be able to search the site, which provides a good range of resources. Of particular interest here are those which relate to the use of the IWB.

PRACTICAL TASK PRACTICAL TASK **PRACTICAL TASK** PRACTICAL TASK **PRACTICAL TASK**

We will now work through an example of finding IWB resources for a Key Stage 2 geography lesson using the TRE. If the focus is 'Rivers' then the following process could be adopted.

The drop-down boxes should look as in Figure 8.1.

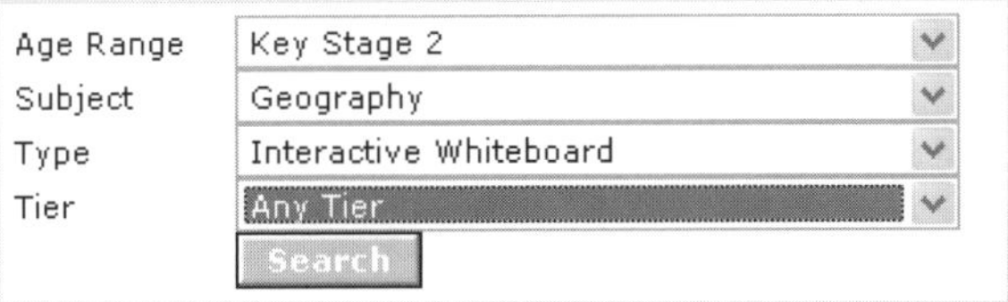

Age Range	Key Stage 2	∨
Subject	Geography	∨
Type	Interactive Whiteboard	∨
Tier	Any Tier	∨
	Search	

Figure 8.1. The search tools on the TRE

The drop-down box labelled 'Tier' merely refers to the stage of development that the resource has attained and it is often best to use the 'Any tier' option. This is because partially developed resources can be further developed to meet your own specifications and requirements, and also because the fact that the author considers it a work in progress does not mean it is not a useable resource. Once the various criteria have been specified, by selecting from drop-down menus of options, the query can be submitted, resulting in a list of 'results'. Each 'title' contains the resources themselves: often Excel documents, IWB presentations, PowerPoint files or some form of multimedia; instructions relating to their use or details of their development, reviews and a series of little icons that can be checked against a key to indicate specific areas of relevance.

At this stage in your search you will only be able to see the small icons and the principal link, which is the leading piece of text, underlined and highlighted in blue. Look down the list of results and identify the item entitled 'river photo animation'. If you click on the hypertext title for this item you will be taken to a window which contains an extended description and all the other elements referred to above. Click on the filenames in the section marked 'materials' in order to access the resources themselves.

An appropriate follow-up activity would be to attempt to identify IWB resources for sessions that you have taught or will teach as part of your school placement.

A significant feature of the TRE is that it provides supportive resources that can be used with most, if not all, major brands of IWB. There are other banks of information and resources which are provided by manufacturers, or those who support manufacturers. These free resources are often of very high quality but are, inevitably, proprietary in their nature. A typical example of this can be seen for the Smart Board™ at **http://education.smarttech.com/ste/en-gb**. Here you will also find advice and case studies, which are equally as valuable and informative as the direct resources and the software. Promethean users can find similar resources on that manufacturer's community portal, at **www.prometheanplanet.com/uk/**

Combining the use of the IWB and the internet with your class on placement

Adding hyperlinks

One of the keys to using the internet in any capacity, including with the IWB, is having an appreciation of the way in which the internet can operate seamlessly with other aspects of your computer software. A good example of this is the creation of hyperlinks. The creation of a hyperlink within Windows-based software can be illustrated by using the generic example of placing the BBC website into a PowerPoint screen. The text 'click here for the BBC website' is written on the slide. This is then highlighted and right-clicked. The option 'Hyperlink' is selected and once this has been achieved the dialogue box shown in Figure 8.2 is displayed.

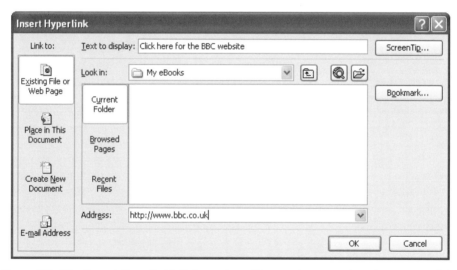

Figure 8.2. The 'Insert Hyperlink' dialogue box. (Screenshot reproduced courtesy of the Microsoft Corporation™.)

You can then type the location of the site or document that you want to add the hyperlink to into the 'Address' box. Once the address has been confirmed and you have clicked 'OK', you will see that the text that you had highlighted has been converted to a hyperlink. The same process could be applied to a photograph, a piece of clip art or even the content of a cell in a spreadsheet. You only need to remember that the most recent versions of Microsoft Office require you to hold down the 'Ctrl' key while clicking on the link in order to activate it.

This is a useful feature as it enables you to use the IWB and its associated features with online content. Some content can be best used by cutting and pasting it into your project. However, internet-based content is of more use when you are using live or regularly updated information. An example of this is a webcam or weather forecasts. Creating a link to online content is also an efficient way of incorporating individual teaching programs (ITPs) into you sessions.

Interactive teaching programs

ITPs are pieces of software designed to be used by individual children or by a teacher in front of a whole class. There is good deal of online content dedicated to this type of resource. In particular, in 2002 the Primary National Strategy website (a subsidiary of the DfES Standards site) devised many ITPs that could be used for whole-class starters or plenaries in numeracy lessons. This is indeed a valuable resource and offers a wealth of good quality interactive teaching materials. These ITPs can be accessed at: **www.standards.dfes.gov.uk/primary/publications/mathematics/itps/**

There are a number of other good examples of interactive material to be found on the internet. For instance, it is worth accessing the BBC's 'Revisewise' site, which can be found at **www.bbc.co.uk/schools/revisewise**. This has a range of content in the core areas based on the national tests at Key Stage 1 and Key Stage 2. The Key Stage 2 science section of this site is at **www.bbc.co.uk/schools/revisewise/gigaflat/rw_chscience/default.shtml?pool=all8**. We would recommend that you have a quick look at this site and the link above. You will see that the focus for this is an individual child. However, using this form of program with the whole class or with a group can be a good way of stimulating question-and-answer sessions or providing you with a structure to your introduction or plenary.

Copyright and internet safety

The internet offers a magnificent range of opportunities for the children and staff alike. However, there are some well recognised and widely reported hazards that the unwary could become ensnared in. We have chosen to include the two most common of these in one section. We don't wish to be alarmist but we do feel obliged to mention these so that you are in a position to protect yourself, the schools in which you work in and, most importantly, the children that you work with. Almost all schools will have policies for both these areas. We would urge you to ensure that you are familiar with these in order to be able to make the appropriate decisions.

Schools should have an acceptable use policy (AUP) for the use of computing technology in school. This should be your first point of reference. Often schools expect all users, regardless of age, to sign that you understand and will comply with the AUP. The AUP will state quite clearly what constitutes acceptable use of email, the internet and instant messaging software. It is imperative that on arrival in school you ensure that you are acquainted with the AUP. This will be one of many sets of rules that you will have to become familiar with in a short space of time. However, this is time well spent. If, having read and signed the AUP, you are still unsure about what is acceptable use of the internet, then it is always best to check with other members of staff, possibly, in the first instance the ICT co-ordinator. Becta offers advice at the following address: **http://schools.becta.org.uk/index.php?section=is&catcode=ss_to_es_pp_aup_03&rid=11087**. For a more detailed perspective, the following document can be downloaded in PDF format, again, from Becta: **www.becta.org.uk/corporate/publications/documents/BEC6190%20Dev%20School%20Pol%20Rev%20AWLR.pdf**

Copyright issues are, to some extent, more complex. It is a sophisticated and dynamic area of the law. This is particularly the case in the area of online publications where precedents continue to be set as the technology develops. Due to the complexity of the area there is a risk that copyright law can be infringed in good faith due to ignorance. However, this ignorance does not serve as a defence. As with AUPs it is important that you are sufficiently familiar with the school policy/law within the area to make appropriate decisions as to how you use the content that you have collected from online sources. It is outside the scope of this book to offer any detailed advice. It is important that you are able to operate within the guidelines offered by the law. Again, we draw your attention to the information offered by Becta. The address is: **http://schools.becta.org.uk/index.php?section=is&catcode=ss_to_es_pp_le_03&rid=10357**

A SUMMARY OF KEY POINTS

After reading this chapter you should understand the following:

> **fully effective use of the internet with IWBs is dependent on the appropriate technology;**
> **searching can be refined to support your own and the children's learning;**
> **databases such as the National Whiteboard Network can provide a useful source of both professional development and teaching resources;**
> **you should always ensure that you are familiar with school acceptable use policies and relevant copyright legislation.**

Useful websites

www.bbc.co.uk
http://education.smarttech.com
www.free-picture-graphic.org.uk/
www.google.co.uk
www.nwnet.org.uk
www.youtube.com
http://en.wikipedia.org

9

Complementary technologies

By the end of this chapter you should:

- have an understanding of the variety of peripherals that can be used with an IWB;
- have some ideas of how to use an electronic microscope with an IWB;
- be aware of how a digital video camera complements the use of an IWB;
- know about voting systems and how they can be used with children in a classroom.

Professional Standards for QTS

This chapter addresses the following Professional Standards for QTS:

Q7, Q8, Q14, Q17, Q23

Introduction

There is an ever-increasing variety of peripheral devices that can be attached to an IWB. This chapter examines just a few of the most notable technologies that are presently on the market and gives some suggestions for their use. At the same time it outlines how each technology complements the IWB and is complemented in its own turn by the connection. Student teachers (and indeed qualified teachers) often express their apprehension of attaching a device to an IWB, for fear that the technology will prove temperamental or that a lack of experience on their part will result in difficulties likely to compromise their teaching.

Exciting and creative work occurs from using equipment like cameras, microscopes and video cameras in conjunction with an IWB. To avoid difficulties and to overcome any lack of confidence with any technology, you should undertake to experiment or 'play' with it, in order to discover how it works. By doing so you will find that you can easily anticipate the kind of problems that may occur in the classroom, but be assured that this kind of equipment is normally very robust and simple to employ.

Many children thoroughly enjoy using ICT equipment of this nature and will not hesitate to press all available buttons and will want to explore the device in detail. The motivational benefits to this type of learning quickly become evident when observing children using technology like this. However, having allayed any residual fears about bringing technology into the classroom, you will have to develop strategies to manage children's enthusiasm in order to ensure the reliable operation of the equipment and the integrity of your teaching objectives.

For example, digital cameras have many settings and unsupervised exploration of the various controls can cause these to be changed, creating the potential for difficulties at a later stage. It is a good idea to establish the prepared settings and ensure that you can recognise if these have been changed by the position of dials or the status of lights or other switches. It is often difficult to locate even the most basic functions, such as turning the flash on or off, if you are not familiar with that particular brand and model of camera.

Imaging devices – digital cameras and scanners

Digital images are referred to throughout the course of this book. With the increasing sophistication of technology it has become much easier to incorporate the use of the digital camera in the classroom. Indeed, it is now desirable for even early years children to learn how to operate a digital camera as part of their introduction to ICT-based learning. The IWB offers an excellent viewing medium for these pictures. Moreover, a child is able, via the whiteboard, to select images, change their dimensions, rotate or move them and even make elements of photographs transparent. Put another way, routines and operations that can be difficult to achieve in complex applications like photo editors, can now – with a little preparation – be taken for granted and achieved with astonishing speed.

Scanners are particularly useful in the classroom when paired with an IWB. It is very easy to use the scanner to import images from a text (copyright permitting) and enlarge them for all the class to see. This facility solves the problem of trying to show a colour image from a small book to a group of 30 or more children. They can also be used to translate the results of activities that children have conducted with tangible media into an electronic document that can be then analysed or combined with others to create a larger resource on the IWB.

CLASSROOM STORY **CLASSROOM** STORY **CLASSROOM** STORY **CLASSROOM STORY**

Vince is nearing the end of his final placement and has supervised a group of children in a local studies project. In the course of this project the children had been on walks around the village and visited local landmarks such as shops, the local church, residential roads and green spaces. In small groups children have produced presentations on each of these landmarks, incorporating photographs, old and new, drawings, pieces of text and a number of simple 'artefacts' obtained during their visits. Vince scans these before hanging them on the wall and places them onto a slide of an IWB presentation. This slide uses a simple aerial plan of the village and each scanned image is reduced to the size of a thumbnail at the proper location on the plan. Vince is then able to discuss the routes that he had taken with the children, asking them to recall things that they had seen or heard on the journey. At stages, as the various landmarks are encountered along this route, the images are resized and the children who made them discuss their display with the rest of the class.

Using digital microscopes with an IWB

A digital microscope allows a child to access the microscopic world and view the results electronically via a PC screen. If that PC is connected to an IWB, the subject under magnification will consequently be displayed for all the class to see. A digital microscope is usually very easily connected to a PC via a universal serial bus (USB) port. Many microscopes offer the option of a hand-held mode, in which the microscope can be removed from its stand and pointed at things. This enables the user to manipulate the equipment and magnify objects that would have previously been inaccessible: the child's own eye or a freckle, for example.

The facility to take snapshots or even movie clips, when an object of interest is discovered, adds another dimension to the microscope tool. Images can then be studied in detail without having to worry about accidental movement and can be saved or manipulated on the IWB by using the software that comes with the microscope. This software typically offers tools that allow children to add paint effects and even sounds. A microscope of this nature is usually greeted with shrieks of delight by the children and its use in a lesson proves to be exploratory and exhilarating.

Figure 9.1. A digital microscope

CLASSROOM STORY **CLASSROOM** STORY CLASSROOM STORY **CLASSROOM STORY**

Student teacher Jason was teaching a Year 5/6 class of children about the different parts and functions of a flower as part of a series of science lessons looking at green plants; his learning objectives were based on the National Curriculum for Science Programme of Study Sc 2, Life Processes and Living Things (DfES,1999, p83).

Jason started the lesson by using a website resource: www.ngfl-cymru.org.uk/vtc/factors_plant_growth/ eng/ Introduction/default.htm

This activity required the children to come to the board and drag and drop the correct label, e.g. 'sepal' or 'anther', to the correct part of the plant. Jason then proceeded to the next segment of the lesson in which he moved from a virtual to tangible learning experience. Jason distributed a bunch of flowers among the class who then faced the task of carefully dissecting and labelling each part in order to progress and consolidate the learning from the IWB lesson starter. To help them, and in order to encourage the children to raise further questions, Jason asked one child to place their dissected flower under the digital microscope; the magnified pictures were then displayed on the IWB. The children then proceeded to undertake a detailed observational pencil drawing of each part of the plant using their own dissections and the magnified images on the whiteboard as inspiration. The children tried to apply the correct label to each plant part as required. At the end of the lesson Jason and the children collaboratively annotated the magnified images of the plant with their correct names, which they then used to assess whether they had accurately identified parts on their own drawings.

REFLECTIVE TASK
- Consider what benefits the use of an IWB has in the previous classroom story.
- Why was it important to give the children real flowers to examine – why not just download photographic images of plant parts onto the IWB?

PRACTICAL TASK PRACTICAL TASK PRACTICAL TASK PRACTICAL TASK PRACTICAL TASK
Every primary school should have a digital microscope. On your next school placement locate it and experiment with attaching it to a PC and an IWB. Take the opportunity to explore the equipment and test out its tools before using it in a lesson.

Digital video cameras

Advances in technology, accompanied by decreasing costs, have made the production of digital movies a realistic activity for primary schools. Indeed, the use of digital video and movie production by children has been steadily gaining momentum. Of particular note is the increasing popularity of small, hand-held devices that can be manipulated by very young children in order to record a short movie. These devices are so intuitive that children can start with very little prior instruction and only moderate levels of supervision. Typically a camera will record up to three minutes of continuous digital images and sound and once the film has been recorded it can be uploaded directly onto a PC. This is normally achieved by placing the device into a docking station that is attached to a PC, and which can be detected as though it were any other kind of memory disk.

The software that accompanies these types of cameras is sufficiently simple to allow the children to edit their movies and to introduce basic scene transitions and effects. What is more, once children have become more familiar with digital movie creation, software extensions can be used in order to tackle some more ambitious tasks. There is currently an increase in using digital movie equipment to produce animations, for example. In particular, children are using clay sets to make props and characters which are animated using stop-motion techniques.

Figure 9.2. Digital video camera

- **Go to the following website:** www.tsof.edu.au/Research/Reports03/bassham.asp. **On this site you will find lots of examples of clay animation work that has been carried out in the primary classroom. Watch some of the video exemplars in order to begin to understand and investigate this type of work.**

CLASSROOM STORY **CLASSROOM** STORY CLASSROOM STORY **CLASSROOM STORY**

Student teacher Phoebe was discovering that her Year 5 class were finding it hard to play together at lunch times. Upon returning to class to start afternoon teaching sessions, Phoebe found that her lessons were delayed because she had to intervene in ongoing disputes. This was unsettling for Phoebe and disturbing for the children; it was also a frustrating scenario as it resulted in a bumpy transition between playtime and fresh learning situations. Phoebe decided to tackle this issue using ICT.

In the first of two related lessons Phoebe issued the children with hand held digital movie cameras. Working in pairs, she asked the children to record each other describing incidents and dilemmas which caused them to argue. These interviews were then shown to the rest of the class via IWB. A lively and wide-ranging discussion ensued as to how these dilemmas might be resolved.

Phoebe commenced the next lesson by showing the previously completed interviews. She then placed the children into small groups and asked them to compose a role play showing how these conflicts could be solved. The role plays were recorded using the digital movie cameras and shown to the rest of the class via the IWB. At various points both the teacher and the children could pause the movie to highlight key points in the plays and to consider how they could be improved. Additional key words for inclusion were listed using the interactive whiteboard pens. The IWB allowed the whole class to view all the plays and enabled a constructive discussion to ensue; the collaborative nature of this evaluation would not have been an option if using a PC monitor.

With the help of the teacher the children then edited their movies to join their initial interviews outlining dilemmas with the role play that proposed a solution. This recording was then used by Phoebe and the class as material for a school assembly that tackled conflict.

REFLECTIVE TASK
ᴚƎ⅃⅂Ɔ∃⅃⅃ɅƎ Ⱶ∀ƧK

This classroom story is not just about movie making and ICT; indeed, it highlights the cross-curricular nature of ICT. Make a list of all the different areas of the curriculum this small case study incorporates.

CLASSROOM STORY **CLASSROOM** STORY CLASSROOM STORY **CLASSROOM STORY**

Year 6 had recently been much concerned with looking after and improving their school environment as part of their geographical studies. Student teacher Arum decided to ask the children to make a video movie that would persuade the rest of the school that they too could help make the school area a better place to learn. Working in groups, the children listed a variety of issues that were giving them cause for concern, ranging from litter around the school to the traffic problems caused by too many cars trying to park close to the school grounds.

Using hand-held movie cameras, the children proceeded to film the hazards, with each group of children filming evidence on two separate issues. On their return to the class the group uploaded their movies on to a PC and interspersed them with additional movie clips of the children explaining each hazard and persuading their audience why these issues needed to be addressed. As the editing process was conducted on the IWB, the whole class was involved in the evaluation of the effectiveness of various parts of the movies, they were all able to take a role in the editing decisions and could participate in the editing process. The completed movies were used on parents' evening to demonstrate concern for the environment and to encourage the adults to work in partnership with the school.

Interactive voting devices

Interactive voting devices are hand-held controllers – like the remote control for a TV – that allow data to be sent from the handsets to a receiver. These data, the responses of the handset owners, are then displayed by a PC. Interactive voting devices can be used to enhance an IWB session, allow children to give and 'see' instant feedback to sets of questions where it is more desirable to canvass whole-class opinion than to focus on the work or ideas of a single child.

Typically every child in a class will control a handset, which allows them to answer questions that arise in the course of an IWB session. If you are having trouble envisaging this scenario it is useful to think of the 'Ask the audience' situation on *Who wants to be a millionaire?*. The results of the vote are then organised into graphs and charts and can be displayed in various ways or studied in detail later. Sometime the handset itself incorporates an LCD display that can give instant feedback to an individual user.

Interactive voting devices give teachers information on how well children understand a particular question and can therefore be very helpful for assessment and monitoring purposes. The teacher is given statistics that provide information on whole-class performance in the form of percentages of right and wrong answers, providing some measure of the teacher's own success in conveying a point. Some systems (including the Promethean device) offer a facility where questions that are shown on the IWB are only revealed for a limited time before moving onto the next. This can be useful in preparing classes for national-test-like timed situations.

Case studies (Holt, 2005) that have explored the practicalities of using these devices suggest that they offer motivational benefits to children and give the opportunity for all of the children in a class to answer a question and receive instant feedback on their choice of answer. Voting systems allow shy children and those who are reluctant to contribute in front of the whole class a way to answer a question without having to verbalise it. It also is a way for the whole class to feel that they are involved in an activity, for children do not have to wait to be chosen by the teacher to answer a question.

Voting systems can be used in many different types of teaching situations. The most obvious use that springs to mind are their application to mental starters in mathematics lessons, which often consist of questioning and rely on a series of rapid responses. However, they can also be used to help children consolidate their knowledge across the whole curriculum. For example, children could use a voting device to show their ability to recognise a verb or a noun. Voting systems can also be used to gather strength of opinion on PSHE issues; they could be used to gather views on the effectiveness of a story or to poll opinion on local issues like the closing of the local swimming baths.

PRACTICAL TASK PRACTICAL TASK **PRACTICAL TASK** PRACTICAL TASK **PRACTICAL TASK**

Go to the website: www.evaluation.icttestbed.org.uk/learning/research/primary/technology/interactive_voting_systems. **This site contains some case studies on the use of interactive voting systems. Access some of them and read them to increase your understanding of their use.**

CLASSROOM STORY **CLASSROOM** STORY **CLASSROOM** STORY **CLASSROOM STORY**

Year 5 were studying fractions in mathematics. The class had been learning how to solve various fraction problems throughout the week and student teacher Roger now wanted to analyse how far the children had progressed with the concepts involved. Roger formulated a multiple-choice set of questions. The questions were displayed on the IWB for all the class to view and Roger used the system's facility to move automatically to the next question.

The instant feedback on the votes of the children gave some interesting information. Roger realised that some of the children had forgotten a few of the concepts visited earlier in the week. One issue in particular, the difference between numerators and denominators, caused several incorrect answers. He decided that this issue could be easily remedied so he reminded the children of the correct names for each part of the fraction before he proceeded any further with the rest of the questions.

Upon returning to the questions, the rest of the answers revealed that a small group of children were confused when it came to simplifying factions. From this information, Roger appreciated that this issue could be further explained to these children, while the rest of the class moved on to tackle the new concepts he had planned for that day in the main part of the lesson.

REFLECTIVE TASK

- **Consider how an interactive voting system might influence assessment and your short-term planning.**
- **How could an interactive voting system complement the use of an IWB?**

Webcams

Webcams used in conjunction with interactive whiteboards can add an interesting dimension to lessons. A webcam is a camera that sends streaming video or regular snapshots of whatever is in its range of vision to a computer. As its name suggests, the webcam is normally used to add live video or image content to a website. Webcams can typically be assigned an IP address, a series of numbers that locates it on a computer network and allows anybody to access it from a web browser.

There are now webcams placed all over the world that can be accessed and used in the classroom. For instance, if children are making a study of the weather around the world they can access real-time images of the weather in the country they are studying. If those pictures are displayed using a projector, the whole class can share in this cinematic experience. Alternatively, a group of children could be given the task of investigating the weather in several locations by conducting a web quest and accessing several different webcams via the use of the internet.

Of course, webcam content can be incorporated into IWB presentations as well. In fact, the IWB allows you to integrate online content into your teaching in a much more seamless way than is possible if you are using a mouse and keyboard. Your navigation of the World Wide Web is much clearer to your audience because you are physically activating the hyperlinks with your finger or your stylus. You are also able to annotate over the webcam image, high-lighting features or following moving elements within the picture with your pen tools.

Go to the website www.earthcam.com. **Investigate some of the available webcams that could be used in the classroom. Consider how an IWB could add value to a task of this type in comparison with conducting it using a data projector and a pull-down screen.**

Streaming webcams that give uninterrupted video as opposed to cameras that supply an image that is updated every few minutes give the opportunity to conduct video conferencing with children in different schools. Webcam views can be projected onto an IWB, making it possible for children to see enlarged images of each other and even the entire class and their teacher. The IWB opens up the webcam conferencing experience from pupils sitting in pairs in front of a PC to whole classes sharing a joint experience. With the use of a microphone, speakers and a webcam of their own, the children in your class can interact with those in other schools.

Video conferencing can be further enhanced by using products like Microsoft Netmeeting. This offers the facility to type messages to each other and to share files over the internet, e.g. work produced in Microsoft Word or PowerPoint, and even share a virtual whiteboard where pictures can be drawn and manipulated or images and text copied and pasted onto the board and then annotated.

There is not room here to discuss in great detail about this sort of product other than to say that this sort of work is achievable with older primary children and wherever this author has delivered this sort of learning experience it has resulted in a very successful and exciting lesson for the children. Visit the website listed at the end of the chapter if you wish to find out more about this product.

When using webcams there are some health and safety considerations to be aware or. If visiting a webcam to access real-time images elsewhere in the world, make sure that you have accessed it first and that you know that it is appropriate for children to view. Webcams give live images so a teacher can never entirely anticipate what the children will see. With this in mind, it is often useful to have a number of alternatives researched and available. If one is not working, or not showing anything of interest, you can then quickly switch to another.

If the children you are working with become involved in a video conference you will need to check that they have parental permission to be involved in an activity of this nature. If you need more information about safety issues it is advisable to visit the British Educational Communications and Technology Agency (Becta), where they are detailed clearly; the website address is given at the end of the chapter.

IWBs and future developments

As we approach the end of this book it is hoped that you now have more of an understanding of the potential of your IWB. At this point it might be appropriate to ponder how your IWB might be put to use in the future. One development is that IWBs with rear projection equipment might become more affordable. This sort of whiteboard offers the same function-ality but locates the projector behind the whiteboard screen, thereby preventing the user creating shadows or blocking the projected image.

In addition, with the increase in the sophistication and affordability of wireless technology, wire-less devices are becoming more and more evident in the primary classroom. Wireless interactive graphic tablets are now being produced by Promethean and Smart Technologies™. Wireless tablets or 'slates' allow a teacher or a child to control the IWB from anywhere in the classroom and this removes the necessity for someone to stand in front of the board, which can obstruct the view of your audience. It also addresses health and safety issues deriving from standing in front of a projector that can dazzle and flickers.

Hand-held and mobile devices also offer great potential for the future. Let us think for a moment about the capabilities and potential of mobile phones. Mobile phones and their use are currently somewhat frowned upon in educational establishments. However, phones now have inbuilt cameras that can capture both still and moving images. Many phones are equipped with Bluetooth wireless technology that enable them to 'talk' to other phones, per-sonal digital assistants (PDAs) and computers.

It is relatively easy to take a movie with your mobile phone and upload it to a Bluetooth-enabled PC connected to an IWB for the class to view. With this sort of technology, the idea of producing films becomes more and more immediate, easier and increasingly cheap. For more information on Bluetooth, access the website listed at the end of the chapter.

The above is just one example of how you might use your IWB; however, what you do with the technology is also up to you and your creativity. As you become an expert user of your IWB, numerous possibilities for its use might spring to mind – what you need to do is to try out, experi-ment, explore and value your ideas and see if they will produce new learning opportunities. Avoid becoming stale in your use of your IWB; be inventive in your learning journey and that will enable you and your children to stay motivated and keep your lessons fresh and up to date.

A SUMMARY OF KEY POINTS

As a result of reading this chapter you should now be aware of the following:

> the range of peripheral devices that can be used with an IWB;
> how to use some of these devices in a classroom;
> where to learn more about the peripheral devices which you are not entirely confident in using;
> that you need to adopt a creative, exploratory stance to technology to keep your IWB use current and fresh – all technologies can diminish in attraction if their use becomes a routine that never changes.

Useful websites

www.playdigitalblue.com/home/
The Digital Blue website shows you their selection of digital microscopes and video camera.

www.taglearning.com/
Shows digital movie cameras and associated products.

www.microsoft.com/windows/netmeeting/

Visit this website if you wish to know more about online conferencing.

http://devschools.becta.org.uk/index.php?section=te&rid=9930&PHPSESSID=e630942d821a00494
a377f0cb63a032d

Becta has a huge website. The above address will take you to the relevant section on webcams and how to use them safely with your class.

www.bluetooth.com/bluetooth/

Learn more about Bluetooth wireless technology.

Animation websites
www.tech4learning.com
www.animationforeducation.co.uk

Interactive voting systems
www.prometheanworld.com/uk/
www.quizdom.co.uk/

Quizdom Interactive Voting System

www.pearsonncs.com/cps/

CPS (Class Performance System)

www.avrio.co.uk/shop/educlick.htm

Educlick Interactive Voting System

www.interactive-education.co.uk/geneeus.htm

GeneeUs Interactive Voting System

References

Becta (2003) *What the Research Says about Interactive Whiteboards.* Coventry: British Communications and Technology Agency.

Becta (undated) *How to Use Webcams Safely in Schools.* Available at: **http://schools.becta. org.uk/index.php?section=is&catcode=ss_to_es_tl_uor_03&rid=9930** (accessed 06.10.06).

Buzan, T. (1991) *The Mind Map Book.* New York: Penguin.

Carter, A. (2002) *Using Interactive Whiteboards With Deaf Children.* Birmingham Grid for Learning. Available from: **www.bgfl.org/bgfl/custom/resources_ftp/client_ftp/teacher/ict/ whiteboards/index.htm** (accessed 08.04.06).

Clark, S. and Cooper, S. (2003) *Showing, Telling, Sharing: Florida School for the Deaf and Blind.* EDCompass Online Community for Education using Smart Products™. Available from: **education.smarttech.com/NR/rdonlyres/303DED40-9E94-4C05-9BA2-AED4404B1AF5/0/ CustCaseStudyFloridaSchoolForTheDeafBlind.pdf** (accessed 19.04.04).

Coffield, F., Moseley, D., Eccleston, K. and Hall, E. (2004) *Learning Styles and Pedagogy in Post 16 Learning, a Systematic Review.* Learning and Skills Research Centre. Available from **www.lsda.org.uk/files/PDF/1543.pdf** (accessed 14.10.04).

Crapper, S. (2002) *Developing Interactive Teaching.* North Islington Education Action Zone. Available from: **www.virtuallearning.org.uk/iwb/Why_IWB_work_for_us.pdf** (accessed 07.04.06).

Cuthell, J. P. (2005) *Seeing the Meaning. The impact of interactive whiteboards on teaching and learning.* Proceedings of WCCE 05 Stellenbosch South Africa. Available from: **www.virtu-allearning.org.uk/changemanage/iwb/Seeing%20the%20meaning.pdf** (accessed 04.04.06).

DfES (1999) *The National Curriculum. Handbook for primary teachers in England.* Key Stages 1 and 2. London: DfES Publications.

DfES (2000) *The National Mathematics Strategy.* London: HMSO.

DfES (2004) *Excellence and Enjoyment: Learning and Teaching in the Primary Years.* London: QCA Publications.

Dunn, K., Dunn, R. and Price, G.E (1975–1997) *Learning Styles Inventory.* Lawrence: Price Systems.

Gardner, H. (1999) *Intelligences Reframed: Multiple Intelligences for the 21st Century.* New York: Basic Books.

Graham (2003) *Switching on Switched Off Children*. Shrewsbury: St Giles CE Primary School. Available from: **www.virtuallearning.org.uk/2003research/Switching_Switched_Off.doc** (accessed 07.04.06).

Goodison, T. (2002) Learning with ICT at Primary Level: Pupils' Perceptions. *Journal of Computer Assisted Learning*, 18, 282–295.

Holt, M. (2005) *Evaluating the Contribution of Activote within the Classroom*. Available from: **www.evaluation.icttestbed.org.uk/learning/research/primary/technology/interactive_voting _systems** (accessed 15.09.06).

Kress, G. (2000) 'Multimodality', in Cope, B. and Kalantzis, M. (eds) *Multiliteracies: Literacy Learning and the Design of Social Futures*. London: Routledge.

Latham, P. (2002) *Teaching and Learning Primary Mathematics: The Impact of Interactive Whiteboards*. North Islington Education Action Zone. Available from: **www.beam.co.uk/pdfs/RES03.pdf (accessed 18.04.06).**

Lee, M. and Boyle, M. (2003) *The Educational Effects and Implications of the Interactive Whiteboard Strategy of Richardson Primary School: A Brief Review*. Richardson Primary School. Available from: **www.richardsonps.act.edu.au/RichardsonReview_Grey.pdf** (accessed 19.04.06).

Levy, P. (2002) *Interactive Whiteboards in Learning and Teaching in Two Sheffield Schools: A Developmental Study*. Department of Information Studies, University of Sheffield. Available from: **www.dis.shef.ac.uk/eirg/projects/wboards.htm** (accessed 03.04.06).

Miller, D.J., Glover, D. and Averis, D. (2005) *Developing Pedagogic Skills for the Use of Interactive Whiteboards in Mathematics*. Glamorgan: British Educational Research Association. Available from: **www.keele.ac.uk/depts/ed/iaw/docs/IAWResearch.pdf** (accessed 15.06.06).

National Whiteboard Network (2004) *Interactive Whiteboards*. Available from: **www.nwnet.org.uk./pages/rev_imp/teachers.html** (accessed 08.04.06).

North Islington Education Action Zone (2002) *Why Interactive Whiteboards Work For Us*. Available from: **www.virtuallearning.org.uk/whiteboards/Why_IWB_work_for_us.pdf** (accessed 13.10.06).

Potter, F. and Darbyshire, C. (2005) *Understanding and Teaching the ICT National Curriculum*. London: David Fulton.

QCA (1998) *Curriculum Guidance for Key Stage 1 and 2: Design Technology*. London: QCA Publications.

Sharp, J. G., Byrne, J. and Bowker, R. (2006) *VAK or VAK-uous? Lessons in the trivialisation of learning and the death of scholarship*. Paper presented at the British Education Studies Association Second Annual Conference, Bishop Grosseteste College, Lincoln, 30 June–1 July.

SMART™ Technologies (2006) Using Microsoft Office Applications with SMART™ Board software. Available from: http://smarttech.com/media/services/quickreferences/pdf/english/ InkAwareQR.pdf(accessed 03.01.07).

Smith, A. and Call, N. (2000) *The ALPS Approach: Accelerated Learning in Primary Schools*. Stafford: Network Educational Press Ltd.

Smith, H (2001) *SmartBoard™ Evaluation: Final Report*. Maidstone: Kent NGFL. Available from: **www.kented.org.uk/ngfl/ict/IWB/whiteboards/report.html#top** (accessed 04.04.06).

Sternberg, R. J. and Grigorenko, E. L. (2001) 'A Capsule History of Theory and Research on Styles', in R. J. Sternberg and L. F. Zhang (eds).

Sternberg, R. J. and Zhang, L. F. (eds) (2001) *Perspectives on Thinking, Learning and Cognitive Styles*. Mahwah, N.J.: LEA.

Warren, C. (undated) *Interactive Whiteboards: An Approach to Effective Methodology*. Available from: **www.virtuallearning.org.uk/iwb/index.html** (accessed 07.04.06).

Index

acceptable use policy (AUP) 83
access 33–4, 57–8, 64
action buttons 68–9
ACTIVboard 7–8, 82
active learning 44
ACTIVprimary 7–8, 15, 24–5
ACTIVstudio 24–9
   adding content 26–7
   manipulating content 27–9
   mouse mode 12
   overview 7
   tools 25–6, 27
adding content
   ACTIVstudio 26–7
   SMART Notebook 22–3
Advanced Search 79–80
ALPS:Accelerated learning in Primary Schools (Smith and Call) 61
animations 62, 67–8, 89, 95
Annotate over Windows 15–16
Annotation mode 15
annotations
   stability 15, 16
   to typeface 23, 29, 61, 64
aspects 2
Attachments 20
audio 66

backgrounds 27, 57
BBC 35, 83, 84
BBC news 35
Becta (British Educational Communications and Technology Agency) 83, 84, 93, 95
Blank button 3
Blind 21
Bluetooth 94, 95
Boyle, M. 48
brainstorming 61
Buzan, T. 61

calibration 5, 7
Call, N. 61
Camera 26
Carter, A. 47
Clark, S. 48
Class Performance System 95
classroom organisation 33, 46
clay animations 89
clicking 12–13

clone 23, 26
collaboration 46
colour 27, 57
Comic Sans 57
compositions 65–6
constructivist paradigm 44
context menus 13–14
Cooper, S. 48
copy/paste 21
copyright 20, 77, 84
creating documents 21
curriculum objectives 52–3, 54
Customise 58–60
Cuthell, J. P. 42, 44, 48

Dale, Edgar 47
deaf children 47
Deconstruct Word 28
design mode 25
DfES, evaluation of resources 52
DfES Standards 56–7, 83
dialogue 46
dice-rolling 26
differentiation 56–7
Digital Blue 94
digital cameras 86
distort 27
dragging 12–13
Draw shapes 26
Drawing freehand 27
drawing mode 14–17
Dunn, K. 42
DVD players 3
dyslexia 57

e-credits 52
early years children 48, 69–70
Educlick Interactive Voting System 95
efficiency 43
engagement 41–2
enhancing learning 44–6
equality of opportunity 33–4
evaluation 52–62
exploratory paradigm 44
eye filters 57

familiarisation 37–8
fans 3
fill colour 27
flipchart view 24–5, 26

fonts 57
freehand drawing 15, 27
freehand to typed 23, 29, 61, 64

Gallery 20
Gardner, H. 42
GeneeUs Interactive Voting System 95
Google 76–7, 78, 79
Graham, K. 46
grammar 48
grouping 23, 24
guidelines 37

hand-writing development 48
Headline History 55–6
headphones 3–4
hyperlinks 24, 82–3

ICT multimodality 35
ICT teaching 35–6
ICT, using 35–6
images, still 77
imaging devices 86
individual educational plans 34, 57
individual/group tasks 34, 37–8
Ink Aware 64, 66
Inspiration 61
installation 2, 33
interaction, levels of 45
interactive teaching programs 56–7, 70–4, 83
interactive voting devices 90–1, 95
internet
    maps 78
    safety 83, 93
    searching 76–7
    still images 77

Kar2ouche 53, 62
keyboards 6, 8
Kidspiration 61
kinaesthetic learning 42–3
Kress, G. 35

Latham, P. 50
layers 24
learning, enhancing 44–6
learning styles 42–3
Learning Styles Inventory 42
Lee, M. 48
Levy, P. 42, 43, 46
Life Processes and Living Things 88
lines 22
location 4, 32–4, 46
Lock in background 28
Lock in place 24
LOGO 44

Macromedia Flash 67
Make Tickertape 28
manipulating content
    ACTIVstudio 27–9
    SMART Notebook 23–4
maps 78
media 35
memory sticks 76
mental warm-up 34, 36
microscopes 87–8, 94
Microsoft Excel 70–1
Microsoft Netmeeting 93
Microsoft PowerPoint 45, 66–70
    early years children 69–70
Microsoft Word 15–16, 63–6
Miller, D. J. 45
mind-mapping software 61
mirror 2
mobile phones 94
modes
    changing 15, 16, 25, 28
    modality and 11
motion paths 67–8
motivation 41–2
mouse mode 11–14, 27
multi-path presentations 68–9
multimodality 35
Multiple Intelligences 42

National Mathematics Strategy (2000) 34
National Whiteboard Network 46, 80
navigation 21

online conferencing 93, 94
opening documents 21
Order 24
organisational strategies 32
overlap 28

pace of lessons 43–4
paste 21
Pencil 29
pens 14–16
percentage view 64
planning 50
play, learning and 42
plenary sessions 34, 38
point and drag 48
pointing 12–13
practical benefits 49–50
presentation mode 25
Primary National Strategy 83
Promptheanworld website 18
Properties 24

re-proportion 28
readability 57

rear projection 93–4
Recognise 23
Recognise Text 29
Recorder 6, 8, 69–70
records of learning 38
remote control 2
resize 27, 28, 71
resources
    children's reaction 60–1
    compatibility 54–5
    curriculum objectives 52–3, 54
    customising 58–60
    differentiation 56–7
    evaluation 52–62
    inventories 53
    usability 54
    websites 49
    see also internet
Revisewise 83
RGB ports 2, 3
right clicks 13–14
rotate 27, 28
Ruler 26
rules 37

safety 83, 93
satellite photographs 78
saved work 49–50
saving documents 21
scanners 86
Schoolzone 53
screen-menu 2–3
search engines 76–7
seating 33
selecting 22
Selector 22
session elements 34
shapes 22
simulation software 62
Slide Sorter 20
SMART Board 5–7
    resources 82
SMART Notebook 20–4
    adding content 22–3
    manipulating content 23–4
    side panel 20
    tools 20–2
SMART Player 6
SMART Recorder 6
Smarttech website 18
Smith, A. 61
Smith, H. 42
Snapshot 21, 26

software 7–8, 19–20, 61, 62
Sound Recorder 69–70
speakers 3–4
special educational needs 33–4, 47–8, 57, 58
spotlight 7, 8, 65–6
still images 77
supported didactic teaching 45
switch 2
Symbol 61

Teacher Resource Exchange 81–2
Teachers Tools 28
text
    formatting 22, 29
    freehand to typed 23, 29, 61, 64
thinking skills 44
toolbars 6, 8, 58–60, 64

undo 21
upside down images 2
USB cables 4
Useful Tools 26

VAK model 42–3
VGA cables 3
video cameras 88–90, 94
video conferencing 93, 95
video, incorporating 77–8
video ports 2, 3
visually impaired children 48, 58
voting devices 26, 90–1, 95

Warren, C. 46
webcams 92–3
websites
    animations 89
    dyslexia 57
    evaluation 52, 53, 60–1
    history 55–6
    interactive teaching programs 83
    resources 49, 62
    science 88
    still images 77
    voting devices 91
whole-class sessions 34, 36–7
Wikipedia 84
wireless connections 75–6, 94
wireless tablets 94

You Tube 77

zoom 21